▶ **Political Cyberformance**

DOI: 10.1057/9781137577047.0001

## Other Palgrave Pivot titles

Lorann Downer: Political Branding Strategies: Campaigning and Governing in Australian Politics

Daniel Aronoff: A Theory of Accumulation and Secular Stagnation: A Malthusian Approach to Understanding a Contemporary Malaise

John Mohan and Beth Breeze: The Logic of Charity: Great Expectations in Hard Times

Carrie Dunn: Football and the Women's World Cup: Organisation, Media and Fandom

David R. Castillo, David Schmid, Dave Reilly and John Edgar Browning (editors): Zombie Talk: Culture, History, Politics

G. Douglas Atkins: Strategy and Purpose in T.S. Eliot's Major Poems: Language, Hermeneutics, and Ancient Truth in "New Verse"

Christophe Assens and Aline Courie Lemeur: Networks Governance, Partnership Management and Coalitions Federation

Katia Pilati: Migrants' Political Participation in Exclusionary Contexts: From Subcultures to Radicalization

Yvette Taylor: Making Space for Queer-Identifying Religious Youth

Andrew Smith: Racism and Everyday Life: Social Theory, History and 'Race'

Othon Anastasakis, David Madden, and Elizabeth Roberts: Balkan Legacies of the Great War: The Past is Never Dead

Garold Murray and Naomi Fujishima: Social Spaces for Language Learning: Stories from the L-café

Sarah Kember: iMedia: The Gendering of Objects, Environments and Smart Materials

Kevin Blackburn: War, Sport and the Anzac Tradition

Jackie Dickenson: Australian Women in Advertising in the Twentieth Century

Russell Blackford: The Mystery of Moral Authority

Harold D. Clarke, Peter Kellner, Marianne Stewart, Joe Twyman and Paul Whiteley: Austerity and Political Choice in Britain

Jonas Campion and Xavier Rousseaux (editors): Policing New Risks in Modern European History

Amelia Manuti and Pasquale Davide de Palma: The Social Organization: Managing Human Capital through Social Media

Piyush Tiwari (editor): The Towers of New Capital: Mega Townships in India

DOI: 10.1057/9781137577047.0001

palgrave▸pivot

# Political Cyberformance: The Etheatre Project

Christina Papagiannouli
*University of South Wales, UK*

palgrave
macmillan

DOI: 10.1057/9781137577047.0001

First published 2016 by
PALGRAVE MACMILLAN

Palgrave Macmillan in the UK is an imprint of Macmillan Publishers Limited, registered in England, company number 785998, of Houndmills, Basingstoke, Hampshire RG21 6XS.

Palgrave Macmillan in the US is a division of St Martin's Press LLC, 175 Fifth Avenue, New York, NY 10010.

Palgrave Macmillan is the global academic imprint of the above companies and has companies and representatives throughout the world.

Palgrave® and Macmillan® are registered trademarks in the United States, the United Kingdom, Europe and other countries.

ISBN: 978-1-137-57705-4  EPUB
ISBN: 978-1-137-57704-7  PDF
ISBN: 978-1-137-57703-0  Hardback

A catalogue record for this book is available from the British Library.

A catalog record for this book is available from the Library of Congress.

www.palgrave.com/pivot

DOI: 10.1057/9781137577047

*In memory of my father (1949–2014) and sister (1978–2015)*

DOI: 10.1057/9781137577047.0001

# Contents

List of Illustrations                                    viii

Acknowledgements                                           ix

Preface                                                     x

1   A Short Organum for Cyberformance:
    The Internet as an Apparatus of
    Communication                                          1
    1.1   Introducing the 'cyber turn': from
          #Hamnet to #Dream40                              2
    1.2   All the world's a (cyber)stage:
          cyberformance as theatre                         6
    1.3   Cyberformance characteristics:
          liveness and interactivity                      10
    1.4   From Tahrir to Taksim: cyberformance
          as a performative                               13

2   Towards an Online Community-Engaging
    and Participatory Theatre: Participation,
    Interaction and Engagement                            19
    2.1   Towards a democratic theatre: the
          'radicalization' of National Theatre
          Wales                                           23
    2.2   Intermedial interculturalism: *Life
          Streaming* and *Call Cutta in a Box*            29
    2.3   Towards a public theatre: cyber-street
          theatre, domestic theatre and
          activist theatre                                35

DOI: 10.1057/9781137577047.0001

3  The Etheatre Project: The Director as
   Discussion Facilitator                              44
   3.1  Cyber-adaptation: *Cyberian Chalk
        Circle*                                        49
        3.1.1  Staging *Cyberian Chalk Circle*         58
   3.2  Cyber-ethnotheatre: *Merry Crisis and
        a Happy New Fear*                              62
   3.3  Cyber-collaboration: *Etheatre Project and
        Collaborators*                                 67
   3.4  Directing absence: strategies of co-presence
        embodiment on cyberstage                       75

Conclusion: Political Cyberformance. Past or Future?   83

Bibliography                                           90

List of Websites                                       113

Index                                                  117

DOI: 10.1057/9781137577047.0001

# List of Illustrations

3.1  Text log of CCC2, Part B (2011)                    54
3.2  Webcam avatar at UpStage 11:11:11                  61
3.3  Whales and birds drawn to demonstrate
     positive natural migration                         74
3.4  Grusha's half-covered face                         76
3.5  Grusha's fragmented body                           76
3.6  Simple line drawings of Grusha and Michael         78

▶

# Acknowledgements

It would not have been possible to complete this book project without the support, help and contribution of many people, of whom, however, for lack of space only a few could be mentioned here. First of all, I would like to express my deep gratitude to my PhD supervisory team, especially Dr Ananda Breed and Dr Dominic Hingorani, and to my thesis examiners, Professor Andy Lavender and Dr Roshini Kempadoo. I wish to thank Helen Varley Jamieson and the UpStage team for their contributions to the Etheatre Project, Ayesha Chari for editing and proofreading my thesis, as well as Dr Annie Abrahams, Øystein Ulsberg Brager, Professor Steve Dixon, Helgard Haug, Marcus Lilley, John E. McGrath and Dries Verhoeven for participating in the project's interviews and inspiring my work. Special thanks to all Etheatre (cyber-)collaborators: Evi Stamatiou, Prodromos Tsinikoris, Ann Cross, Tom Mangan, Dr Sarahleigh Castelyn, Anca Donzi, Suzon Fuks, Charis Gavriilidis, Marischka Klinkhamer and Ilinca Tamara Todorut. Finally, this book is dedicated to my family and to the memories of my father, Dr Nikolaos Papagiannoulis, and my sister, Dr Katerina Papagiannouli.

# Preface

Written from a practice-based perspective, this book examines 'cyberformance' – the genre of digital performance that uses the Internet as a performance space – as a political practice from the viewpoint of the theatre director. The Etheatre Project comprises a series of experimental cyberformances that aim to reconsider the characteristics of theatre and the methodologies of directing theatre performances within the phenomenon of the remediation of cyberculture. Based on my PhD research at the University of East London titled The Etheatre Project: Directing Political Cyberformance (2010–14), this study focuses on the use of Internet platforms as theatrical, rehearsal and performance spaces and explores the interactive and political potentials of online theatre, questioning the boundaries of these in-between spaces and the spatial experiences they cause.

The main motivation for starting this project came from two primary pragmatic observations and needs. The first of these was my increasing use of the Internet to establish direct (and often instant) contact with my homeland, Greece. The second was the need for low-budget performance spaces and research tools, as this self-funded project started in the middle of the global financial crisis. The similarity between this global economic crisis and the British monetary crisis of the 1970s, which resulted in the art crisis as well as the acceleration of the politicization of theatre following Margaret Thatcher's art cuts during the 1980s, was evident. Thus arose the need to look at the new medium of the Internet for cheaper ways of producing

DOI: 10.1057/9781137577047.0004

theatre performances. Although new technology is considered to be expensive, the Internet offers a range of free-of-charge tools and platforms to promote creativity and collaboration. These two factors, along with my Greek origin and my classical theatre education, have greatly influenced the process and outcome of this book and research.

In September 2010, I used the term 'Etheatre', which later became the project's title, to name the phenomenon of online theatre ignoring at the time the existing terms used to define these practices. From the public introduction of the Internet and the World Wide Web in the mid-1990s, artists and researchers have attempted to name and define online theatre practice, using terms such as 'cyberdrama' (Murray, 1997), 'cyberformance' (Jamieson, 2000, defined in Jamieson, 2008, p. 2; see also Jamieson, 2013a), 'digital performance' (Dixon, 2001, defined in Dixon, 2007), 'cyber(-)theatre' (Causey, 2003; Dixon, 2004), 'virtual theatres' (Giannachi, 2004), 'networked performance' (Green, Thorington and Riel, 2004), 'telematic performance' (Saltz, 2004), 'cyberperformance' (Causey, 2006), 'cybertheater(s)' (Nusberg, 1969; Chatzichristodoulou, 2006, 2010), 'digital practices' (Broadhurst, 2007) and 'hyperformance' (Unterman, 2007). The variety of terms used to explain this phenomenon demonstrates the diversity of online practices, the varied intermedial characteristics, the lack of agreement of definitions between scholars, researchers and artists, as well as the rush to gain authorship over online performance.

Janet H. Murray coined the term 'cyberdrama', recognizing it is 'only a placeholder for whatever is around the corner' (1997, p. 271), to describe the emerging form of storytelling by the use of computers and games. In *Hamlet on the Holodeck: The Future of Narrative in Cyberspace* (1997), Murray discussed the interactive and participatory potentials of cyberdrama, suggesting a variety of existing and imagined storytelling forms – some of which at the time were science fiction but now exist (Jamieson, 2008, p. 25) – in order to investigate whether cyberdrama can transpose the truth of the human condition as truly and as beautifully expressed as in theatre (Murray, 1997, p. 274). However, cyberdrama refers to virtual forms of text-based storytelling, a form of play script, rather than to the performance itself.

In 2003, Matthew Causey replaced 'drama' with 'theatre', defining cybertheatre as a 'performance created with the aid of new media and computer technologies'. He used the term to critically examine computer-based performances, questioning the importance of liveness

DOI: 10.1057/9781137577047.0004

in such a mediatized form: 'Cyber-theatre, not unlike film and television, does not rely on the presence of a live actor or audience and an argument can be made that many examples of cyber-theatre might be better described as interactive film/TV, installation art, new media art, or electronic communications' (Causey, 2003, p. 341). Thus, although Causey identifies the blurred boundaries between online theatre and interactive film – a demarcation that, sometimes, is difficult to identify and analyse – he generalizes the definition of cybertheatre as a non-live performance genre instead of examining the differences between the two forms of net art.[1]

In 2004, Steve Dixon reused the term cybertheatre to describe his project *Chameleons 3: Net Congestion* (2000), produced by the Chameleons Group, a UK-based multimedia performance research company founded in 1994 by Steve Dixon, Paul Murphy and Wendy Reed. *Net Congestion* ironically aimed to investigate the interactive character of the Internet in theatre, demonstrating the importance of a live actor and audience in cybertheatre (see Dixon, 2003):

> My work as director of *The Chameleons Group* (since 1994) has experimented with Artaudian and digital conceptions of the 'double', and has explored the development of new interactive cyber-theatre paradigms, including a series of performances where online audience members in a chat room directed and spontaneously 'wrote' a performance for ten actors (in an empty theatre) to perform in real time. (Dixon, 2006, p. 68)

The Artaudian experiment allowed online audiences to direct the performers and write their dialogues in real time during the performance, using cyberspace as a cyberstage – Dixon soon realized the power of real-time interactive communication between the performer and the 'disembodied' audience (Dixon, 2003, 2004).

In an article titled 'Adventures in Cyber-Theatre (or the Actor's Fear of the Disembodied Audience)', Dixon critically reviewed the *Net Congestion* project by analysing the 'liveness, bodyless and spaceless' issues of the cyberstage, as well as its interactive character, concluding that 'although the actual physical distance between performers and audience is increased, interactive communication changes the nature of the spatial barrier since the spectator seems as present and often as prominent as the performers within the performance space of the computer monitor proscenium' (2004, p. 118). In a later article, Dixon (2006) revived the discussion on the notion of presence and co-presence in cybertheatre, as evident from the dialogue between physical and virtual bodies and

DOI: 10.1057/9781137577047.0004

physical and virtual spaces, which gave rise to the term 'virtual touch' to describe moments of real contact and intimacy between the actors and the audience across the network. What remains to be asked, however, is how a theatre director can assure and strengthen this virtual touch of co-presence in online theatre. (I discuss examples of virtual touch in Chapter 2 and co-presence tactics in Chapter 3.)

In 2006, Causey returned to the term cybertheatre, this time in order to acknowledge liveness as an important characteristic of online performance, recognizing the interactive potentials of 'computer-aided performance', 'a more practical term than *cyber-theatre* or *postorganic performance*' (2006, p. 48; emphasis added). He also used 'telepresent performance' and 'cyber-performance' to describe digital practices (Causey, 2006, pp. 48, 83). Similarly to Dixon, Causey turned to Antonin Artaud's 'body without organs' and the 'double' to analyse the virtual: 'What I am modelling is a recapitulation of Artaud's double, but the function of the double collapses in the event of the virtual. Everything is in cyberspace and thus nothing is ever not-this, not the double, not an illusion nor an appearance' (2006, p. 96; see also Artaud, 1958 [1938]).

During the same year, Maria Chatzichristodoulou (aka Maria X) also used the term cybertheater(s) in her research, entitling her thesis 'Cybertheaters: Emergent, Hybrid, Networked Performance Practices and Visions'. Focusing on the origins of the term cybertheater – Chatzichristodoulou (2012, p. 1 and 2014, p. 20) credits the term to the Russian kinetic arts group Dvizjenije – the aim of her research was to articulate this emerging form as a new performance genre, by the appropriation and redefinition of the term cybertheater, under the philosophical umbrella of Gilles Deleuze and Félix Guattari's notion of the non-linear, non-hierarchical rhizome. Although Chatzichristodoulou (2006) defined cybertheater – a transdisciplinary genre that ontologically exists between theatre, performance/live arts, cinema, Internet and computational technologies – as '*performance* practices that make use of the Internet both as a distribution medium and as a space/stage for the development of dramatic (re-/inter-)actions and co-creations between their diverse agents', she does not engage in discussions around intermediality (i.e., interaction between different media) and intermedial studies (I study cyberformance as an intermedial form of theatre in Chapter 1).

Chatzichristodoulou borrowed the term 'networked performance' – coined by Jo-Anne Green and Helen Thorington (of the Turbulence Project[2]) and Michelle Riel to define 'real-time, embodied practice within

DOI: 10.1057/9781137577047.0004

digital environments and networks' and 'embodied transmission' (see Green et al., 2004) – to describe performances that employ the Internet (2010, pp. 3, 18; see also Chatzichristodoulou, 2012, p. 4 and 2014, p. 22).

Green, Thorington and Riel (2004) used the term to originate a blog of the same title to chronicle current network-based practice, aiming 'to obtain a wide-range of perspectives on issues and uncover commonalities in the work'; the online source revealed the explosion of creative experimental performances as affected by the rapid advancement of mobile technology.

In *Virtual Theatres: An Introduction*, Gabriella Giannachi used the word 'virtual' to analyse twenty-first-century computer-arts practices, 'in which everything – even the viewer – can be simulated' (2004, p. i), to conclude that 'there is not one virtual theatre, but many. This is not only because of the variety of virtual art forms that can claim a certain degree of theatricality, but because the medium of virtuality itself acts as a theatre, a viewing point of the real' (2004, p. 151). Hence, virtual theatre is used here as a broad term in the quest to classify and study different computer-based forms of theatre, such as virtual reality theatre, hypertextual performances and cyborg theatre. Referring to a variety of artists and groups, including, *inter alia*, Blast Theory, Forced Entertainment and Guillermo Gómez-Peña's La Pocha Nostra, Giannachi places virtual theatre in the category of arts that give 'serious consideration to technology as a *form* of art' (2004, p. 1; emphasis in the original), defining it as a theatrical form that 'remediates' (i.e., represents one medium in another) – a theory Giannachi borrows from Jay David Bolter and Richard Grusin's *Remediation* (2000; Giannachi, 2004, p. 4). According to Giannachi, this process of 'remediation' implies a certain degree not only of 'intertextuality and metatextuality, but also of intermediality and metamediality' (2004, p. 5). As she explains, 'the etymology of the word "technology", *tekhnē*, indicates that technology is also an art, a craft, and shows how profoundly technology and art are linked. Just as art has repeatedly advanced through technology, technology has, via art, acquired aesthetic signification' (2004, p. 1).

In *The Politics of New Media Theatre*, Giannachi studies political practices of performance and new technologies, focusing on the topics of globalization and surveillance. Although she explores theatre as *hacktivism* and draws on the fact that 'on the Internet notions of authorship, individualism, privacy and even freedom of speech need to be (re-)defined' (2007, p. 14), Giannachi's explorations cover new media

DOI: 10.1057/9781137577047.0004

theatre in a broad way, ranging from body art and bioart to cloning, genomics and architecture.

In 2005, Benjamin Unterman focused on the use of computers in performance making and used the term 'computer-mediated theatre' in his Master's thesis, which comprised an analysis of space, audience and presence in online theatre. Two years later, Unterman suggested the term 'hyperformance' in a conference paper, 'The Audience in Cyberspace: The Lessons of Hyperformance', defining hyperformances as 'live events presented across computer networks' and describing them as 'the most striking forms of the mediatisation of theatre' (2007, p. 1). He focused on the participatory and more active character of hyperformance and concluded that 'this added reliance on interactivity[,] and the breaking down of the barriers between artist and audience, makes hyperformance a unique and valuable new direction in intermediatised theatre' (2007, p. 1).

In 2000, Helen Varley Jamieson coined the term 'cyberformance' (see Jamieson, 2008, pp. 2, 30, 34) in an attempt to find a more appropriate and useful word to describe her experimental work in collaboration with Desktop Theater. Desktop Theater describes itself as 'an ongoing series of live theatrical inventions' (2000). The project, also called 'Internet Street Theater', was created by Adrienne Jenik and Lisa Brenneis and operated from 1997 to 2002. After trying to combine a variety of terms including online, Internet, theatre and performance, Jamieson arrived at the portmanteau word *cyberformance* by blending *cybernetics* and *cyberspace* with *performance*. In spite of her collaborators being called Desktop Theater, Jamieson (2012a) chose the term 'performance' over 'theatre' because 'at that time "theatre" seemed like a very heavily laden word that was tied to very boring mainstream theatre that is about bland entertainment'. (For this reason I find it necessary to define theatre in Chapter 1.)

Jamieson's definition of cyberformance, as explained in her thesis 'Adventures in Cyberformance: Experiments at the Interface of Theatre and the Internet' (2008, pp. 13–34), contextualized it within the fields of networked performance, digital performance, telematic performance and theatre. David Z. Saltz, scholar and principal investigator of Virtual Vaudeville: A Live Performance Simulation System, used the term 'telematic performance' to describe 'live multi-site performance events' that make use of video streaming technologies to live broadcast distributed performers (2004, p. 128). The Virtual Vaudeville Project is an interactive three-dimensional system that helps simulate live performance events from any historical period (Virtual Vaudeville,

DOI: 10.1057/9781137577047.0004

2004). According to Saltz, a computer user's interaction is a performance by itself, tracing the similarities of computer technology and theatre in Artaud's 'virtual reality' and Brecht's 'remarkable anticipation of Internet culture' (2004, pp. 121, 128; see also Artaud, 1958 [1938]; Brecht, 1964b [1932]). Saltz also rightly pointed out that the use of computers in the performing arts challenges the boundaries between performance disciplines, between scholarship and creative practice and between live and mediatized performances. Similarly, Andy Lavender too used telematic performance to discuss the dramaturgical possibilities of such interactive telematic events that 'involve two or more geographically distinct sites, linked by telecommunications technology' (2006, pp. 552, 558–59) in terms of 'telematic collaboration' – another term that I will later discuss as 'cyber-collaboration' (in Chapter 3).

Despite deficiencies in the definition, as performers can be remote and/or proximal, Jamieson (2008) offers a precise characterization of cyberformance for future artists and researchers to discuss, question and modify. According to Jamieson, cyberformance is 'live/ly' (i.e., although it is mediatized, it takes place in real time); it is 'situated in cyberspace', and thus 'digital' and 'distributed' geographically; it 'has attitude' (a result of the 'unexpected' nature of online performance), and is 'resourceful' (in terms of technology) and 'transparent' (i.e., it 'does not pretend to be real'); yet, it remains 'unfinished' owing to its interactive character (2008, pp. 34–40).

Thus, telematic performance (use of streaming and video conferencing applications) and hyperformance (use of hypertext) can be considered to be subcategories of cyberformance, which in turn can be seen as a subcategory of digital performance and networked performance because it only refers to digital practices that use the Internet. Accordingly, cyberdrama can function as a subcategory of cybertheatre, and cybertheatre, in turn, can be regarded as a subcategory of virtual theatre. Furthermore, cybertheatre can be understood as the theatrical genre of cyberformance, distinguished from other performance arts, such as music, dance and fine art installations.

I chose to reuse the term cyberformance, instead of etheatre, as it has been well defined in contemporary literature in the field, and in works of researchers, and describes online practices clearly. Jamieson has influenced the work and research of Chatzichristodoulou, Unterman and other cyberformance researchers, including the author, by collaborating with and offering the UpStage platform (co-curated by Jamieson and other cyberformers and students) to artists and researchers through the annual UpStage Festival. Following the cyberformance characterizations described, I aim to continue in this book the discussion that Jamieson introduced so well with her research, focusing on the political character of cyberformance that derives from its interactive character.

This comprehensive study of online theatre terms and their definitions uncovers two key characteristics of cyberformance common to all of them. The first is the context of mediation, which is primarily studied through Artaud's *Theatre and Its Double* (1958 [1938]) in combination with philosophical theories. A significant number of scholars and artists have re-studied and re-interpreted Artaudian theories in the context of digital culture (Popovich, 1999; Sakellaridou, 2007). In addition to Causey (2006), Dixon (2006) and Saltz (2004), Broadhurst (2007) too has studied Artaud's 'body without organs' to analyse the absent presence of the virtual body in 'digital practices' – her phrase to refer to performance practices that 'prioritize such technologies as motion tracking, artificial intelligence, 3-D modelling and animation, digital paint and sound, robotics, interactive design and biotechnology' (2007, p. 1).

The second, and perhaps more important, common characteristic is that '[the terms] foreground, in different ways, the notion of liveness. Indeed, liveness is one of the most vital characteristics of theatre and performance art' (Chatzichristodoulou, 2012, p. 4 and 2014, pp. 22–23) – a trait that digital technologies have turned into a problem. Auslander (1999) criticized and challenged the conventional view of performance theory, which characterizes the relationship between the live and the mediatized as one of opposition: Auslander 'found that scholars working in mass media studies, particularly those interested in television or popular music, have dealt more directly and fruitfully with the question of *liveness* than most scholars in theatre or performance studies' (1999, p. 3, n. 5; emphasis added). In the case of online theatre, liveness has a direct relationship with interactivity as audience participation can occur only in the course of live, real-time communication. (I discuss liveness and interactivity as cyberformance characteristics in Chapter 1.)

The originality of this book and the Etheatre Project lies in its consideration of the political character of cyberformance and the use of Brecht's theatrical methodologies in online theatre. Although it explores subject areas that have been already discussed, such as interactivity in cyberspace and the spacelessness, bodylessness and liveness of cyberformance, *Political Cyberformance: The Etheatre Project* studies cyberformance

DOI: 10.1057/9781137577047.0004

through the viewpoint of the practitioner–researcher, more specifically, the theatre director.

Beginning with a historical overview of online theatre that lays the foundation of this monograph, Chapter 1, 'A Short Organum for Cyberformance: The Internet as an Apparatus of Communication', introduces the term cyberformance to discuss the characteristics of online theatre. Looking at cyberformance as the outcome of the intermedial marriage between theatre and the Internet, 'liveness' and interactivity are determined to be key characteristics of cyberformance. The chapter presents a critical comparison between the Royal National Theatre's NTLive *Phèdre* production and Forced Entertainment's 24-hour *Quizoola!*. The case studies demonstrate the importance of interactivity for creating liveness in online theatre. To establish the political character of cyberformance, the chapter investigates emergent economic, social and political implications and interactions of the Internet with physical space and society.

Chapter 2, 'Towards an Online Community-Engaging and Participatory Theatre: Participation, Interaction and Engagement', delves into the use of the Internet in performance making to explore notions of socio-political engagement in online practices and the importance of social networking platforms in public 'conflictual' participation. Key examples of community engagement and audience participation in cyberformance are discussed in the chapter. Particular attention is paid to the National Theatre Wales (NTW) Community blog and the use of the Internet as a space for conflictual participation, as well as the performances of Dries Verhoeven's *Life Streaming* (2010) and Rimini Protokoll's *Call Cutta in a Box* (2008). The performance review locates the Etheatre Project in a lineage of practice, allowing the practical study of online theatre boundaries and characteristics.

Chapter 3, 'The Etheatre Project: The Director as Discussion Facilitator', is an account of the practical work and the adapted directing methodology of the Etheatre Project, under the umbrella of Bertolt Brecht's political theatre theories and practices. It investigates the role of the director as discussion facilitator in cyberformance research and practice. Referring to the *Cyberian Chalk Circle* (2011), *Merry Crisis and a Happy New Fear* (2012) and *Etheatre Project and Collaborators* (2014) projects, the chapter explores the prospects of forming political spaces through performances on cyberstage using Brecht's methodologies and

DOI: 10.1057/9781137577047.0004

theories of directing political theatre, questioning new forms of spatial relationships and dialectics. I conclude with a summary of research findings determined through the methodologies of the Etheatre Project, not only presenting answers to questions I raise at the start of my research but also raising questions that need further investigation to reveal the future of cyberformance. While early discussions of some of the research of this book have been published as papers in the *International Journal of the Arts in Society* and the *ATINER's Conference Paper Series*, this complete monograph contributes to literature knowledge through its focus on the political and dialectical characteristics of cyberformance and the directing strategies followed to meet those parameters. Referring to contemporary examples of online, socio-political and participative theatre performances that took place during the 'cyber turn' in UK theatre (2010–14), the Etheatre Project expands on the use of cyberformance as a medium to negotiate between theatre and the Internet and performance and performatives.

## Notes

1   Net.art is an art movement by a group of artists who coined the term in 1995 to describe their own work. However, as Jamieson notes, 'net.art (or net art or net-art or netart ...) has come to be accepted as encompassing any artistic practice that takes place on or via the internet' (2008, p. 27, n. 23).
2   Turbulence is a project of New Radio and Performing Arts, Inc. (NRPA, 1996). NRPA was founded in New York City in 1981 to foster the development of new and experimental work for radio and sound arts. In 1996, it extended its mandate to net.art and launched its pioneering website Turbulence.org.

DOI: 10.1057/9781137577047.0004

palgrave▶**pivot**

www.palgrave.com/pivot

# 1

# A Short Organum for Cyberformance: The Internet as an Apparatus of Communication

**Abstract:** *The chapter offers an art historical overview of cyberformance as theatre from the Hamnet Players' debut cyberformance of Hamnet to the Royal Shakespeare Company's Twitter adaptation of Romeo and Juliet. Looking at cyberformance as the outcome of the intermedial marriage between theatre and the Internet and comparing the Royal National Theatre's NTLive Phèdre and Forced Entertainment's 24-hour Quizoola! case studies, liveness and interactivity are determined to be key characteristics of online theatre. Drawing on Bertolt Brecht's radio essay (1964b [1932]), Papagiannouli discusses the interactive character of the Internet to conclude that the Internet is the new agora, a meeting point for politics to be discussed and ideas to be shared.*

Papagiannouli, Christina. *Political Cyberformance: The Etheatre Project*. Basingstoke: Palgrave Macmillan, 2016.
DOI: 10.1057/9781137577047.0005.

## 1.1    Introducing the 'cyber turn': from #Hamnet to #Dream40

Research for the Etheatre Project began at a time when the goliaths of UK-based theatre went digital. On 25 June 2009, NTLive¹ – part of the Royal National Theatre in London – broadcast live its production of *Phèdre* to 73 cinemas in the United Kingdom and 200 more round the world. In April and May 2010, the RSC staged Shakespeare's *Romeo and Juliet* on Twitter for its five-week-long staging of *Such Tweet Sorrow* – the 'world's first professional Twitter-based performance of Shakespeare' (Arts Council England, 2012, p. 11). In summer of the same year, the London International Festival of Theatre (LIFT, 2014), under the new artistic direction of Mark Ball, focused on the emergence of digital technology in the world of theatre. Since these productions, a rapidly increasing number of leading art houses and theatre companies have begun using the Internet – including Tate Modern's *BMW Tate Live: Performance Room*, Punchdrunk and Forced Entertainment – forming a wave of UK-based theatre 'cyber turn'.

Besides the vigorous use of the Internet on contemporary British stage, online theatre has a substantial international history that cannot be ignored. On May 2012, Helen Varley Jamieson (2012b) posted on the Furtherfield Gallery community blog a passionate text criticizing the Tate's launch claims about *BMW Tate Live* being an 'entirely new mode of presentation' (see Tate, 2012) and 'the first artistic programme created purely for live web broadcast' (see Tate, 2011). In her blog post, Jamieson (2012b) rightly questioned these claims, offering a short overview of the history of online performance. She pointed out that cyberformance dates back to at least 1994, when fine artists Nina Sobell and Emily Hartzell (1994) launched 'ParkBench', transforming their studio into a 'time-based public Web installation' by creating a weekly, online, live, video-based performance series called *ArTisTheater*. The RSC, too, ignored the rich history of cyberformance and online Shakespearian theatre – from the Hamnet Players' debut cyberformance of *Hamnet* (irc Theatre, Live!!!, 1993), to the SL Shakespeare Company's (2007–08) efforts 'to bring to "Second Life" *live* productions of all of the bard's plays', to the Plaintext Players' (1994–2006) 'live online and mixed-reality performances since 1994', to Maria Chatzichristodoulou's (2006–10) writings and collaborative projects on digital and networked performance – and 'with a little help from Google+' advertised *#Dream40*, its 2013 *Midsummer Night's*

*Dream* production, as an 'innovative digital project' and 'a new kind of play' (Royal Shakespeare Company and Google+, 2013).

The history of cyberformance, as outlined by Jamieson (2012b), highlights the disregard of leading art institutions (for the online performance space) concealed in the advertisement of their digital projects as 'pioneering'. Despite Twitter, Google+, Second Life, multi-user object-oriented (MOOS) environments and Internet relay chat (IRC) channels being different online communication platforms, their theatrical uses share a common *raison d'être*: direct, real-time communication between theatre and its remote, geographically distant audience.

Since 2010 and the Twitter adaptation of *Romeo and Juliet*, the RSC has tried to investigate 'new forms of creating narrative expression' (Collinge, 2011), following a path more interactive than its classic productions by experimenting with digital technology. Six actors, coached and directed by Roxana Silbert, improvised the dialogue of the central characters for *Such Tweet Sorrow*, following the framework of an overall scripted grid that plotted the action of each character. Bethan Marlow and Tim Wright wrote daily missions for each actor, who could then 'act' from wherever they could get online. The missions were delivered each morning, telling the actors how the story would evolve that day, and the actors had to improvise and decide what to say by posting tweets of up to 140 characters (Mudlark, 2010). The tweets, merged and archived in the *Such Tweet Sorrow* public list on Twitter (https://twitter.com/such_tweet/lists/such-tweet-sorrow), compromised the script of the adaptation. However, the live version of the play was created and completed by both the actors' and the audience's tweets. Nearly 6,000 people followed Juliet, and an average of 4,000 audience members followed and interacted with the other characters through real-time hypertext updates and tweets, including videos, pictures, web pages and text logs, posted on Twitter over a period of five weeks (Collinge, 2011).

The 'new forms of creating narrative expression' (Collinge, 2011) that *Such Tweet Sorrow* attempted in 2011 has been existing since 1993. The Hamnet Players – founded by 'semi-professional' actor and computer professional Stuart Harris – 'debuted the concept of participatory Internet Theatre', performing text-based adaptations of classic plays on IRC channels (Danet et al., 2006; irc Theatre, Live!!!, 1993). Brenda Danet et al. (2006) used the term 'semi-professional' to emphasize Harris' former experience as an actor on the festival circuit, raising questions about the underlying causes of his IRC experiment.

DOI: 10.1057/9781137577047.0005

Harris recognized the dramatic potential of IRC and successfully brought together amateur and professional actors from all over the world – mainly London, Tel Aviv, Durban, Slovenia and Oslo – to produce the world's first online version of a Shakespeare play: *Hamnet*, an 80-line parody of *Hamlet* staged on an IRC channel called *#hamnet* (Danet, 2002). The Hamnet Players, perhaps unaware of the publicity potential of such a pioneering enterprise, managed to gain a remarkable amount of attention from conventional media, such as USENET news-groups, American National Public Radio, local television interviews and newspaper coverage in the *Los Angeles Times* as well as the *London Times*. Harris collaborated with Ian Taylor of the RSC for the second production of *Hamnet* in 1994, with Taylor in the lead role (Danet et al., 2006). To mark Shakespeare's 430th birthday, the Hamnet Players performed *PCBeth: An IBM Clone of Macbeth*, a 160-line version of *Macbeth* with visual images (irc Theatre, Live!!!, 1994a). In the second version of *PCBeth* (in July 1994) and in the last project of the company, *An irc Channel Named #desire* (which premiered the same year), based on Tennessee Williams' play *A Streetcar Named Desire*, the Hamnet Players included sound files: 'Sound-bits pertaining to the show will be offered to ppl with sound-capable equipment (i.e. with sound-cards installed)' (irc Theatre, Live!!!, 1994b).

From 1994, the Plaintext Players, an online performance group founded by new media artist Antoinette LaFarge, also performed direct textual mixed-reality improvisations on cross platforms (such as MOOS) to explore new ways of interactive play-writing. Their *LittleHamlet* project, for instance, was a 'reworking of the Hamlet story that inverted text and subtext' to allow 'all of the characters' formerly unspoken needs, fears, and desires [to come] to the fore' (Plaintext Players, 1995). Like Harris' parodies, the Plaintext Players used hypertext to explore classic plays in a comic way:

> **CLAUDIUS:** *Laertes, my dear boy, there's been an unfortunate, er, misunder-*
> *standing ...*
> **LAERTES:** *I demand revenge! ... Who and how was my father killed?*
> *[psst ... it wasn't cancer]*
> **BLOODYGERTRUDE:** *No one lives forever, Laertes ... jeesh ... grow up.*
> **CLAUDIUS:** *... involving a, ah, curtain, and uh ...*
> *[killed by a curtain? But that's absurd!]*
> **LAERTES:** *Yes, yer Malady?*
> *[psst, he wasn't hit by a bus ... heck, we don't got no busses yet]*

DOI: 10.1057/9781137577047.0005

CLAUDIUS: ... *and a no ... He was very nosy, your father.*
BLOODYGERTRUDE: *Anyway, think of the insurance money.*
*[Or do we? Are there Danish busses?]*
CLAUDIUS: *And I didn't do it!*
LAERTES: *Look, I'm seeking ABSOLUTE TRUTH!*
CLAUDIUS: *I didn't do the other thing either!*

– From *LittleHamlet* (Plaintext Players, 1995; emphasis in the original)

Apart from solely text-based platforms, online theatre artists have used avatar-based virtual worlds, such as Second Life, and virtual stages, such as UpStage, for their performances. The SL Shakespeare Company, another professional theatre troupe, used the Internet to 'make Shakespeare cool again!' (SL Shakespeare Company Blog, 2009–10) before the RSC used Twitter for the same reason. According to Geraldine Collinge, the production manager of *Such Tweet Sorrow*, Twitter is 'one way that the story [of Romeo and Juliet] might be told today' (quoted in Cavendish, 2010). The Internet does indeed offer both the opportunity to approach and engage new, and mainly young, audience in theatre as well as the scope to use creative and futuristic tools for storytelling.

Not only professional and amateur artists but also researchers and scholars look at the Internet as a theatre stage. In 2007, artist, researcher and scholar Maria Chatzichristodoulou (aka Maria X), among others, performed *Ophelia_machine* as part of the 070707 UpStage Festival. The play was a textual collage based on Shakespeare's *Hamlet*, Heiner Müller's *Hamlet Machine* and Donna Haraway's *Cyborg Manifesto* (Chatzichristodoulou, 2010, p. 248). Despite the complexity of the avatars, which functioned as puppets in the hands/computer keyboard of the artists, the communication with the audiences was centred on a simple chat-based relationship.

UpStage is a cyberformance stage software produced in 2004 by Douglas Bagnall for the Avatar Body *Collision* (Helen Varley Jamieson, Karla Ptacek, Leena Saarinen and Vicki Smith) cyberformance group (UpStage, 2004). On 7 July 2007 the first cyberformance festival, 070707 UpStage Festival, was organized as a celebration for the launch of UpStage v2. This has since become an annual cyberformance festival, with the 080808, 090909, 101010 and 11:11:11 UpStage Festivals attracting many artists, students and researchers to collaborate and experiment with this platform. The festival's format was broken in 2012 to mark the last possible year the date sequence could be followed and the beginning of DownStage, a new engine to replace the UpStage platform (Eisenbarth,

DOI: 10.1057/9781137577047.0005

2012). The 121212 UpStage Festival took place between 5 and 12 December and consisted of two parts: in the first part, called 'Walking Backwards into the Future' (5–11 December), cyberformances from the previous five festivals were re-performed; in the second part, called 'Testing – 12,12,12' (12 December), new works were produced on UpStage and other online platforms, including VisitorsStudio, mosaika.tv, Waterwheel Tap, Livestream, eTV and the Second Life social environment. The 'Walking Backwards into the Future' section of the 121212 UpStage Festival also served as a stimulus for the Avatar Body *Collision* group to again perform together after five years (they had not performed as a group since 2007; see Jamieson, 2012a).

Prior to the 121212 UpStage Festival, an online global symposium on cyberformance hosted by UpStage, Waterwheel Tap and independent researchers and artists also highlighted the importance of past cyberformances. The 'CyPosium' (as it was called), held on 12 October 2012, aimed to discuss, question and analyse the history of online performance (CyPosium, 2012), by bringing together artists and researchers from different genres – dance, music, theatre, installation and media art – to talk about their cyberformances. This chapter studies cyberformance as theatre, as this originates from the constant effort of theatre artists and researchers to direct and produce Shakespearian performances online and the British 'cyber turn', to determine its key characteristics and define it within socio-political implications and interactions.

## 1.2  All the world's a (cyber)stage: cyberformance as theatre

In 2000, theatre-maker, digital artist and researcher Helen Varley Jamieson coined the term 'cyberformance' to define the form of 'live performance that utilises internet technologies to bring remote performers together in real time, for remote and/or proximal audiences' (2008, p. 34). Borrowing Jamieson's term, this chapter examines how the Internet and the World Wide Web inform the way in which theatre is made in cyberculture – what Andy Lavender defined as 'techne' (2006, p. 551) – by exploring the characteristics of cyberformance and the boundaries of theatre those characteristics negotiate.

Cyberformance is a genre of digital performance that uses the Internet as a performance space or a cyberstage: 'a socio-political in-between

DOI: 10.1057/9781137577047.0005

space and non-space, where the participants are present and absent at the same time in a live and mediatised experience' (Papagiannouli, 2011a, p. 61). For their 2001 Digital Performance Archive (DPA) research project, Steve Dixon and Barry Smith defined 'digital performance' to include 'all performance works where computer technologies play a *key* role rather than a subsidiary one in content, techniques, aesthetics or delivery forms' (quoted in Dixon, 2007, p. 3; emphasis in the original). The 'spaceless', 'bodyless' and 'liveness' characterization of the cyberstage references the binary nature of the materiality and immateriality of cyberspace, whereas its socio-political character references the global nature of online environments (Papagiannouli, 2011b). This dual hypostasis of the cyberstage comes in coherence with the binary computer code (0,1 binary digits), which allows dissimilar features and oppositions to exist at the same time, changing the question from 'to be or not to be' to 'to be *and* not to be'. The in-betweeness of the cyberstage reveals the intermedial character of cyberformance – a *metaxy*, Plato and Aristotle's notion of in-betweeness, that is, a situation in-between different mediums such as theatre and the Internet, theory and practice, and live and mediatized performance:

> The use of computers in the performing arts does not merely add a new tool to an old discipline. It challenges some of our most basic assumptions about performance. First, it blurs the boundaries between performance disciplines. [ ... ] Second, it blurs the boundaries between scholarship and creative practice. [ ... ] Finally, digital technology is challenging the very distinction between 'liveness' and media. (Saltz, 2004, p. 129)

The term 'intermediality' first appeared in print in 1989 to critically describe the use of other media, such as cinema and television, in theatre (Anstey, 2007, p. 2). Since then, the word has been widely used in different contexts and discourses, resulting in the creation of the Intermediality in Theatre and Performance Working Group within the International Federation of Theatre Research (IFTR, 2012) in 1998. The aim of the group is to identify and define the essence of intermediality in theatre and performance by analysing the use of different media in theatre practices. 'Intermedial' is defined here as an in-between space, a mixture of 'spaces, media and realities' (Chapple and Kattenbelt, 2006, p. 12): it is 'about the staging (in the sense of conscious self-presentation to another) of media, for which theatre as a hypermedium provides pre-eminently a stage' (Kattenbelt, 2010, p. 29).

DOI: 10.1057/9781137577047.0005

I draw on Victor W. Turner's (1990) notions of liminality and perform-ance, to highlight how in-betweeness refers here to actual liminality rather than a symbolic transitional state (*'rite de passage'*) in ritual arenas (see also Schechner and Appel, 1990). Intermediality is a key term in this research as it focuses on the interaction between different media – in the case of the Etheatre Project, between theatre and the Internet – where one redefines the other, by learning from each other, as proved by the collaboration between computer scientists and artists for the creation of online platforms such as UpStage and Waterwheel Tap. Challenging some of its most basic assumptions, cyberformance – the outcome of the intermedial negotiation between theatre and the Internet – allows a broader understanding of theatre.

Although Jamieson (2008) introduces cyberformance as a new theat-rical form, she avoids using the term theatre to describe it, recognizing the release of the winds of Aeolus such use could cause in theatre circles. According to Twyla Mitchell, theatre sees computers as 'enemies', fearing that new technology will replace theatre, similarly to humans' fear that computers will replace people, or, in the case of *Matrix*, that avatars will replace humans (1999, pp. 10–11). Apart from the technophobia, thea-tre is 'a very heavily laden word [ ... ], tied to [ ... ] mainstream theatre' (Jamieson, 2012a) and specific aesthetics, which require a certain code of behaviour and procedures. As Jamieson notes, although theatre and performance are at times substitutable, 'the subtle yet crucial differences between *theatre* and *performance* have been the subject of much debate' (2008, p. 19; emphasis in the original). For this reason I find it necessary to define theatre: I use the term *theatre*[2] to describe the *dramatic*[3] art of theatre performance as a whole, including all the acts required for the realization of a theatrical performance, such as the text, the actors, the audience and the space.

Bertolt Brecht defines theatre as a 'live representation' of human inter-actions with an emphasis on entertainment, highlighting the importance of liveness in theatre: '"Theatre" consists of this: in making live repre-sentations of reported or invented happenings between human beings and doing so with a view to entertainment. At any rate that is what we shall mean when we speak of theatre, whether old or new' (Brecht, 1964d [1949], p. 180). Indeed, although the relationship between performers and the audience has experienced radical changes through theatre history, the presence of a live audience relationship is central to the definition of theatre art (Freshwater, 2009, p. 1). However, digital technologies have problematized the recognition of liveness in all kinds of performance, leading to the opposition of live and mediatized performance. According to Philip Auslander, this separation between live and mediatized derives from cultural and historical contingencies rather than from the juxtaposition of their fundamental characteristics (1999, p. 11).

Thus, defining 'live' is essential in this chapter which looks at the term in accordance with Steve Wurtzler's (1992) view of the 'recorded': 'live is premised on the absence of recording and the defining fact of the recorded is the absence of the live' (Wurtzler, 1992, p. 89). In this respect, live performance is any kind of performance that is not pre-recorded for its audience. Consequently, despite the delay that may occur, cyberformance is a live performance owing to its real-time characteristic. Although performers and audiences are distributed, they share a common space – the cyberspace – through real-time online communication. After all, theatre in its poorest form is all about this direct, live communication between the performer and the spectator.

> By gradually eliminating whatever proved superfluous, we found that theatre can exist without make-up, without autonomic costume and scenography, without a separate performance area (stage), without lighting and sound effects, etc. It cannot exist without the actor–spectator relationship of perceptual, direct, 'live' communion. This is an ancient theoretical truth, of course, but when rigorously tested in practice it undermines most of our usual ideas about theatre. (Grotowski, 2002 [1967], p. 19)

Agreeing with the above definition, Chiel Kattenbelt defines theatre as 'the social meeting between performer and spectator in the live presence of the here and now' (2006, p. 33): a 'here and now' that Robin Nelson sees as taking place 'in virtual, rather than, [*sic*] actual space' in cyberformance (2010, p. 19). Although the performers and the audience do not share the same geographical space in cyberformance, Jerzy Grotowski's 'perceptual, direct, "live" communion' (2002 [1967], p. 19) is accomplished through the co-presence of actors and spectators in cyberspace, as this derives from the interactive participation of the audience in real time. According to Ball (2013), 'hyper-connected theatre allows us to reimagine the very nature of a theatrical experience and of an audience by utilising networks to engage people as active participants with a real sense of agency.'

In a more Wagnerian approach, Kattenbelt has argued that 'theatre is a physical hypermedium [a synthesis of disparate creative disciplines, such

DOI: 10.1057/9781137577047.0005

as music, dance, opera, cinema, media art and visual art installation] whereas [ ... ] the Internet is a virtual hypermedium' (2008, p. 23), and suggests, as mentioned earlier, that the former pre-eminently provides a stage to media (Kattenbelt, 2010, p. 29). However, considering that the Internet is a virtual hypermedium, the Internet and its cyberspace, unlike other media, do seem to provide a stage for theatre. The Shakespearian quote 'all the world's a stage' becomes feasible through the Internet which offers 'performative' spaces, such as blogs, social networking platforms, virtual environments and communication applications comprising chat rooms, web cameras and avatars. The term performative is used here to describe the ability of cyberspace to bring into existence a performance act because of its interactive character and to turn into a cyberstage for online audiences. Birgit Wiens rightly underlines that 'it is not enough to interpret the Internet as the "largest theatre in the world"' (2010, p. 108) because it is of greater importance to identify and analyse the emergent economic, social and political implications and interactions of the Internet with physical space and society. The Etheatre Project, focusing on the political character of cyberformance, addresses these implications and interactions.

## 1.3    Cyberformance characteristics: liveness and interactivity

This section studies the main characteristics of cyberformance, liveness and interactivity, as these derive from the intermedial negotiation between theatre and the Internet. I argue that the notion of liveness in cyberformance is directly connected to the interactive and participative character of the Internet, as without real-time engagement the notion of co-presence is weak and, thus, liveness is meaningless. Following Russell Fewster's claim that 'in the context of a broad debate about liveness and mediatisation, however, each production presents its own challenges' (2010b, p. 63), it is worth comparing NTLive's *Phèdre* production with Forced Entertainment's *Quizoola!*, a durational performance generated from a series of questions. In cyberformance, liveness is no longer an aesthetic choice, as in the early experiments of digital performance, but rather a basic trait.

Technology in theatre is not new. Online theatre, like digital performance, is 'an extension of a continuing history of the adoption and adaptation of technologies to increase performance and visual art's aesthetic effect and sense of spectacle, its emotional and sensorial impact, its play of meanings and symbolic associations, and its intellectual power' (Dixon, 2007, p. 40). Many digital performance artists and scholars have argued that the roots of online theatre can be traced back to the *deus ex machina* (Ἀπὸ μηχανῆς θεὸς) of Ancient Greek theatre, the magic lantern of Robertson's phantasmagorias at the Pavillon de l'Echiquier in the 1790s or the revolutionary introduction of electric light in the 1890s (Lavender, 2006; Dixon, 2007; Jamieson, 2008; Oliver, 2013). Matthew Causey has suggested that theatre has always been a 'virtual', 'illusory' space and that there is 'nothing in cyberspace [ ... ] that has not already been performed on the stage' (2006, p. 15). Indeed, although cyberformance is a recent phenomenon, online theatre was conceived before the technology to make it possible even existed.

It was since Richard Burton's 1964 *Hamlet* production, directed by John Gielgud, that artists looked at technology to bring live theatre experience to simultaneous viewers and reach wider audiences, giving rise to what came to be known as 'Theatrofilm' (The Wooster Group, 2006–13). The Broadway production comprising 17 camera angles, recorded and edited into a film, was supposed to have been destroyed after its run for two days in 2,000 movie houses across the United States, making the experience of watching it not much different from what the Royal National Theatre offers with its NTLive. This raises questions about what live streaming and Internet technology offer to theatre today different from what Theatrofilm offered, revealing the importance of real-time interaction and participation in cyberformance.

The case of the *Phèdre* production questions the meaningfulness of the expensive liveness commodity in NTLive, as well as the performance discipline it belongs to, as it broadcasts live and recorded theatre performances to cinemas via satellite in a LiveTV-like manner. Following the live high-definition performances of the Metropolitan Opera in New York (2006), the San Francisco Opera (2006), London's Royal Opera House (2007) and the Berlin Philharmonic Orchestra (2008) on cinema screens across the country (Bakhshi and Throsby, 2010), NTLive became 'the first theatre in the world to film a live performance in high definition and broadcast it via satellite to cinema screens around the world' (National Theatre, 2013–14; see also National Theatre Live, 2009–14). The expensive high-definition *Phèdre* experiment would not have been feasible without funding from NESTA (2013–14) – an independent charity

DOI: 10.1057/9781137577047.0005

with a particular interest in supporting 'research and development of projects that use digital technology to enhance audience reach and/or explore new business models for organisations with arts projects' (Arts and Humanities Research Council, 2012) – and partnerships with the Picturehouse, Odeon and Cineworld chains as well as several independent cinemas.

According to Hasan Bakhshi and David Throsby (2010), both part of the NESTA research team, 'more than 50,000 people' saw *Phèdre*'s digital premiere – an equivalent to the production's total audience number over the play's three-month run – thereby expanding the capacity of the theatre virtually: 'A total of 14,000 people across the UK saw that evening's production [in real time] (excluding those who experienced it at the National itself). A further 14,000 people saw it live across Europe or on the same day in North America (allowing for time zone delays)' (Bakhshi and Throsby, 2010, p. 29).

During the 2013 SPILL Festival of Performance,[4] Forced Entertainment – a UK-based, six artists' theatre company founded in 1984 – followed a more interactive path in a 24-hour version of their *Quizoola!* production. The sold-out performance was webcast live for free, reaching 4,541 online views between 11:59 p.m. on 12 April and 11:59 p.m. on 13 April, from the Barbican Centre on three different websites: Barbican, SPILL Festival and Forced Entertainment. In addition to NTLive's focus on the director's viewpoint, the high-definition streaming of the 24-hour, one-off, ground-breaking theatre project was a simple one-camera live webcast of the event, while the webcast links allowed the audience to follow the tweets of other audience members (see Trueman, 2013). This enriched the live experience of the online audience, who could read posts of offline and online spectators and communicate with each other. Even though the performers did not interact with the audience in real time, the online audience felt extremely engaged with the show because of the sense of audience co-presence on Twitter. This suggests that the sense of co-presence is essential in online theatre, in contrast to other digital forms such as live or interactive cinema.

Forced Entertainment allowed some kind of pre-performance interaction by inviting the audience to send them questions. The number of questions submitted to be part of the performance exceeded 3,000; the 24-hour *Quizoola!* reached 1.8 million Twitter impressions, connecting 58 countries over 6 continents (Forced Entertainment, 2013). Furthermore, the 'marathon' and temporary character of the durational performance

DOI: 10.1057/9781137577047.0005

made it hard for online spectators to drag themselves away from it (see Palgrave Theatre, 2013; Stephens, 2013).

Hence, owing to its lack of immediacy with the audience, the NTLive experience cannot be considered a theatrical one but rather a form of live cinema. In contrast, the use of Twitter in the 24-hour *Quizoola!* performance created a strong sense of theatrical coexistence of the online audience and the company. The theatrical visual freedom in NTLive is repealed as the director of photography controls what the cinema audience views, whereas the general plan of *Quizoola!* allows a more theatrical frame, where the screen becomes the proscenium box. This suggests that some sort of interaction is required in cyberformance for the liveness of experience to be accomplished.

Exemplifying the Internet's collective information distribution, where anyone can tweet or re-tweet information, theatre makers can use the Internet to collect inspiration from their audience during rehearsals (e.g., the call for questions Forced Entertainment announced for its production). Blogs and social media, such as Facebook and Twitter, allow participants to engage with the performance from the very beginning of the planning process; they can also function as instruments of feedback surveys and tools for audience interaction during the actual show. In the #quizoola24 Twitter feed, the audience commented on the show, providing real-time feedback to performers' questions (see Curtis, 2013). The combination of live webcasting and social media virtually extends the performance space, which not only allows geographically distributed audiences to interact or participate actively in an event taking place on the other side of the globe but also allows groups of people unable to travel (e.g., those with physical disabilities) to attend the performance from wherever they are. In keeping with the free culture of the Internet, most live webcastings of theatre performances are offered to online audiences free of charge, allowing the participation of economically weaker audiences and encouraging equality in theatre participation.

## 1.4   From Tahrir to Taksim: cyberformance as a performative

This section looks at the interactive character of cyberformance as a performative, drawing on Bertolt Brecht's radio essay (1964b) [1932]. In particular, it investigates the emergent economic, social and political implications and interactions of the Internet with physical space and society to frame its political character, as suggested by Wiens (2010). The Internet is the new *agora*, a meeting point for politics to be discussed and ideas to be shared. Referring to the examples of the political use of the Internet from the Arab to the Turkish Spring, this section discusses the enlarged distance between 'digital' and 'cyber' technology to conclude that theatre should make use of this interactive online world.

The Internet has been in existence since the 1960s, and has grown into a key communication medium and one of the most powerful tools for generating and sharing ideas and opinions in the twenty-first century, as marked by its recognition by the United Nations as a 'human right' (2011, p. 4). The development of refined mobile technology and the increasing use of mobile devices, such as smartphones, tablets and laptops, have contributed to the growing number of Internet users – a figure that crossed the 2 billion mark during 2011 (United Nations, 2011, p. 4). The invention and growth of the Internet has had a revolutionary effect on the future of information technologies, as consumers have the option of actively interacting by self-publishing information rather than being just passive recipients of knowledge. The United Nations' report suggests that 'unlike any other medium of communication, such as radio, television and printed publications based on one-way transmission of information, the Internet represents a significant leap forward as an interactive medium' (2011, p. 6). The World Wide Web and social media, such as Twitter and Facebook, allow data to be transmitted swiftly and receivers to *comment, share, like* and *debate* information, making feasible Brecht's (1964b [1932]) utopian assertion of altering the radio into an apparatus of communication:

> But quite apart from the dubiousness of its functions, radio is one-sided when it should be two. It is purely an apparatus for distribution, for mere sharing out. So here is a positive suggestion: change this apparatus over from distribution to communication. The radio would be the finest possible communication apparatus in public life, a vast network of pipes. That is to say, it would be if it knew how to receive as well as to transmit, how to let the listener speak as well as hear, how to bring him into a relationship instead of isolating him. On this principle the radio should step out of the supply business and organize its listeners as suppliers. Any attempt by the radio to give a truly public character to public occasions is a step in the right direction. (Brecht, 1964b [1932], p. 52)

Thus, Brecht's creation of a dialectical theatre was 'not intended to be of use to the present-day radio but to change it' (1964a [1932], p. 32). Brigid

DOI: 10.1057/9781137577047.0005

Doherty complements Brecht's 'positive suggestion' of converting the medium (radio) from an 'apparatus of distribution' into an 'apparatus of communication', by highlighting Walter Benjamin's theory of the fundamental distance between the practitioner and the audience as the basis of his (Benjamin's) radio experiment 'crucial failing' (2000, p. 447).

> This passive, and incapacitated attitude of the audience [ ... ] can be changed for the better by an adequate use of the radio. But, still, it is the '*crucial error of this institution to perpetuate in its work the fundamental split between performers and audience, which is belied by its technical foundations.* Any child could tell you [ ... ] that the aim and object of radio broadcasts is to put all kinds of people at any time in front of the microphone.' (Benjamin, 'Reflections on the Radio', 1932, quoted in Werber, 2003, p. 233; emphasis in the original)

Where radio failed, the Internet succeeded: it brought together all kinds of voices in the same space. Owing to its universal appeal and interactive nature, the Internet began to be used politically from the very beginning of its existence, turning into a space for political expression. Similarly to the structure of the Ancient Greek *agora* (i.e., a public gathering space), commercialized Internet has been altered into a marketplace, a meeting point for politics to be discussed and ideas to be shared. As Markus Miessen remarks, 'the rhizomatic, hyperlinked, and non-physical structure of the Web is the new *agora* – an accelerated, co-authored system of shared and co-edited knowledges' (2010, p. 166). The Internet has turned into a tool for participatory democracy ('radical democracy'), a multi-viewpoint medium that allows a more comprehensive picture of so-called truth in relation to the monopolistic, elite-controlled media. As Lincoln Dahlberg and Eugenia Siapera explain, 'through its mythological non-hierarchical network of free information flows, the Internet is seen as offering a perfect "marketplace of ideas", a space for information exchange and individual decision-making free of bureaucracy, administrative power, and other restrictions (bodily, geographical, cultural) of "real" space' (2007, p. 3).

From the uprising at Cairo's Tahrir Square in 2011 to the political protests at Istanbul's Taksim Square in 2013, the World Wide Web has functioned as a space for political mobilization, leading to the question of whether social media can create a revolution, although the Internet's blackout during the course of demonstrations problematized its democratic notion. Here, the Internet becomes what Baz Kershaw (1992) describes as a 'double-edged weapon'; whichever way the weapon cuts, the intention is to 'strengthen the self-determination of the community,

DOI: 10.1057/9781137577047.0005

to contribute to the empowerment of the community within – or against – the dominant socio-political order' (Kershaw, 1992, p. 66).

The political power of the Internet was well demonstrated in Egypt's cyber blackout during the 2011 public unrest, where the government cut off the entire country from the Internet soon after Twitter, Facebook, Google and YouTube were blocked. Although the Internet played a crucial role in public unrest during the Arab Spring – a term used by world media for the revolutionary protests in the Middle East at the beginning of 2011 – and helped spread democratic ideas by shaping political debates (Howard et al., 2011), leading political theorists, such as Chantal Mouffe, support the view that the Internet cannot create a genuine social movement. In an interview with Miessen, on being asked what she thought was an example of actual political mobilization, Mouffe replied: 'When you have a variety of constituencies, including workers and poor people, who become mobilized and organized. Not simply young people on the Internet' (quoted in Miessen, 2010, p. 141).

Although I agree with Mouffe's definition of a social movement, I disagree with the exclusion of the Internet as a space for such political mobilization. The 'potato revolution' in Greece, for instance, demonstrated the social power of the Internet in terms of citizens' self-organization. The phrase was used during March 2012 by the world media to describe the market movement in Greece in protest against rising prices, where the public started to buy potatoes directly from farmers, cutting out the middleman. Potato farmers began the movement as a topical reaction against the market's high prices on account of the middleman; however, it soon grew into a food revolution spreading across the country. Volunteers, educational institutions and town councils started forming online communities, using the Internet as a public space, to meet food needs. Although food markets were set up in offline spaces, the organization of such mass exchange (resulting from the vast numbers of food orders) would not have been possible without the Internet (Lowen, 2012; Henley, 2012). (Interestingly, the potato's revolutionary role is linked with many important historical mass movements, such as the British Industrial Revolution in the nineteenth century and the introduction of the potato to the Greek farmers in Greece by Ioannis Kapodistrias in 1828.)

As mobile phones are superseded by smartphones, smart communities, too, are created and developed in due course, using the Internet as a socio-political platform to reclaim public spaces – both virtual and geographical. The Internet has turned into a menace for power-holders, a publicly controlled apparatus of multi-lies against the absolute truth of controlled mass media as proved by the use of social media during the so-called Turkish Spring. On 28 May 2013, Turkish ecologists had occupied Gezi Park in Istanbul's Taksim Square to protest against the park's demolition. The extreme violence that Turkish police forces used against the protesters detonated larger demonstrations across Turkey, resulting in the death of five citizens and thousands of injuries. The local media – controlled by the government – hushed up the events, leading the protesters to use Twitter to 'fill the gaps left by TV' (Katik, 2013). This only enlarged the distance between the 'digital' and 'cyber', as a clear separation became evident between controlled, government digital media and self-managed public Internet sources, leading to the metaphorical and literal defamation of the medium of the Internet by the power-holders.

Prime Minister Recep Erdogan summarized the Turkish government's views by declaring: 'There is now a menace which is called Twitter. [...] The best examples of lies can be found there. To me, social media is the worst menace to society' (quoted in Letsch, 2013). He later used Twitter, 'the worst menace to society' as a surveillance tool, to label the protesters and moved to arrests. Despite the democratic character of the Internet, there is no doubt that the risk of undemocratic use exists. This is evidenced by the fact that fake Facebook accounts had to be created for the Etheatre Project audience to use (see discussion in Chapter 3). Cyberformance directors and practitioners should acknowledge this issue and protect the anonymity of the participants, especially in projects dealing with political topics.

Brecht's utopian assertion that 'radio is one-sided when it should be two' (1964b [1932], p. 52), and thus should be made to receive as well as transmit, by letting the listener speak and hear and by bringing him/her into a relationship instead of isolating him/her, finds ground in the medium of the Internet. The alteration of the radio into an apparatus of communication, as well as the mass social change Brecht sought through his political theatre, no longer seems unrealistic in cyberculture. As Brecht stated, 'theatre has to become geared into reality if it is to be in a position to turn out effective representations of reality, and to be allowed to do so' (1964d [1949], p. 186). In light of his concerns about the representability of the modern world, I argue that theatre, not only as a type of entertainment but also as a social art, and consequently as a political act which reflects the world we live in, should make use of the interactive online world.

DOI: 10.1057/9781137577047.0005

# Notes

1   The NTLive Project is named after the Royal National Theatre's initials and the word 'live' to highlight its real-time character (available at: http://ntlive. nationaltheatre.org.uk/, accessed 30 December 2013).

2   'Theatre' comes from the Ancient Greek verb θεάομαι-θεώμαι (*theaomai-theomai*, derived from θέατρον or *theatron*), which means to think/see/observe/ watch/look.

3   'Drama' comes from the Ancient Greek verb δράω-δρῶ (*draō-drō*, derived from δρᾶμα or *drama*), which means to act/do.

4   The SPILL Festival of Performance is an 'international festival of experimental theatre, live art and performance presenting the work of exceptional artists from around the globe' and is produced as an initiative of the UK-based Pacitti Company (SPILL Festival of Performance, 2007–14).

DOI: 10.1057/9781137577047.0005

# 2

# Towards an Online Community-Engaging and Participatory Theatre: Participation, Interaction and Engagement

▶

**Abstract:** *Papagiannouli explores participation, interaction and engagement in cyberformance in the context of democratization of theatre (in terms of radical democracy), looking at intermedial interculturalism and community/ public engagement in theatre to locate the Etheatre Project in a lineage of practices. Particular attention is paid to the National Theatre Wales Community blog and the use of the Internet as a space for conflictual participation, as well as the performances of Dries Verhoeven's* Life Streaming *(2010) and Rimini Protokoll's* Call Cutta in a Box *(2008). The chapter also examines the Høyblokka Project's (2010–12) use of the Internet as a memory archive space; Merton and Folds' cyber-street theatre performances on Chatroulette; Jamieson's use of private and public spaces to stream eco-cyberformances; and Field Broadcast's nine-day-long virus-like performances.*

Papagiannouli, Christina. *Political Cyberformance: The Etheatre Project*. Basingstoke: Palgrave Macmillan, 2016. DOI: 10.1057/9781137577047.0006.

Online discussion is an increasingly popular method of engaging in political debate. However, as analysed in Chapter 1, the democratic character of the Internet, in terms of pluralism and freedom of speech, is highly debatable; or, as Robin Nelson remarks, 'the jury on digital culture remains out' (2010, p. 22). Despite its democratic predisposition, the effect of the Internet – as with any other technological breakthrough – depends on its use. According to Marshall McLuhan, 'the serious artist is the only person able to encounter technology with impunity, just because he [she] is an expert aware of the changes in sense perception' (1964, *Understanding Media*, quoted in Shanken, 2009, p. 13). Although I am opposed to McLuhan's suggestive differentiation between the serious and the non-serious artist, I agree with his view about the use of technology. Theatre practitioners should use technology with impunity, leaving the audience to acquire the role of the dialectical spectator in a polyphonic setting.

In this respect, I am not going to engage in a debate about whether the Internet is an enemy or ally for humanity and arts; this has been already discussed before the Internet even existed, on the occasion of the invention of the telegraph and, more recently, the invention of mobile phone technology (Adams et al., 2010). Instead, in this chapter, I focus on the different techniques of the use of the Internet in performance making, for facilitating direct participation of the public in socio-political discourse. Here, participation refers to 'conflictual participation', a form of critical engagement instead of 'a politically motivated model of pseudo-participation' as dealt with by Miessen (2010) in *The Nightmare of Participation (Crossbench Praxis as a Mode of Criticality)* and summarized by Jeremy Beaudry and Bassam El Baroni in the postscript to Miessen's work (2010, p. 256).

According to Clare Bishop (2012, p. 277), participation in arts is connected and runs parallel to the story of democracy: 'Participatory art is not a privileged political medium, nor a ready-made solution to a society of the spectacle, but is as uncertain and precarious as democracy itself; neither are legitimated in advance but need continually to be performed and tested in every specific context' (Bishop, 2012, p. 284). Theatre makers, such as John E. McGrath (2012, 2013), Dries Verhoeven (2012) and Rimini Protokoll (2002–14), use the Internet effectively to democratize communities virtually and find new ways of engaging with audiences, moving away from the elitism of high art.

This chapter draws on Kershaw's definition of 'community theatre' (1992, p. 5) to study examples of public engagement in cyberformance and to question the power of theatre and the Internet in bringing about social change. On the basis of text-based Skype interviews with artists and researchers, I look at the participatory character of cyberformance in terms of community and civil engagement. I provide a critical account of online theatre projects, during the timeframe of research undertaken for the Etheatre Project, to present the different approaches and strategies each cyberformance used to engage a particular community in a certain socio-political context.

In the United Kingdom, 'community theatre' is misinterpreted to mean amateur theatre. Being distinguished from professional theatre, it has earned a negative connotation in theatre circles. Instead, the term 'community-based theatre' or 'community-oriented theatre' has been used to describe what Kershaw defines as 'a theatre of social engagement, a theatre primarily committed [in Brechtian terms] to bringing about actual change' (1992, p. 5) – an actual change not in the way that things are done but in terms of how people think. According to John P. McGrath, 'theatre can never cause a social change,' but 'it can articulate the pressures towards one', by providing a space for people to find voice (1981, p. xxvii). Besides, as James F. English points out, 'community is not a solution to the political problem, but a problem in its own right' (1994, p. 21).

Cyberformance brings community back to its initial purpose: *to commune*, which Mady Schutzman suggests is 'to talk together, to be in close rapport' (2006, p. 139), through democratic but critical participation. The pluralism of theatre changes how people think through critical engagement; that is, according to Ellen W. Kaplan, 'the understanding and communication of experience as distance' (2005, p. 171). This socio-political experience opens new ways of thinking about change (Scott, 1991). To cite a few examples, National Theatre Wales (NTW, 2009–10) used the Internet to give voice to a younger generation and engage the community of Wales in theatre. Verhoeven (2012) brought Western technology to the East to connect the two worlds and share experiences as a commentary to media representation. Rimini Protokoll (2002–14) also connected the East with the West using existing technology to allow interaction between two geographical spaces. The 2010–12 Høyblokka Project engaged citizens of Trondheim, Norway, to collect, archive (in a blog) and embrace in a site-specific performance diverse memories about the landmark old town hospital that was demolished to make way for a modern structure (see Høyblokka, 2010–12), whereas Jamieson (2008, 2012a) (and others) used private spaces such as participants' houses and public spaces such as galleries, libraries and laboratories to stream eco-cyberformances.

This chapter looks at these examples of participatory online practices and the ways in which these cases engage different communities to locate the Etheatre Project in a lineage of practice. Referring to the NTW community blog and the company's productions, I study the term 'radicalization' in a positive way in terms of plural and participatory democracy to discuss the use of the Internet for the re-democratization of theatre. Similarly to the engagement and interaction of the Ancient Greek theatre community, the NTW Assembly programme uses the community blog as a space for the community of Wales to discuss and vote online to run democratically elected projects. Moreover, the use of a chat box and the Twitter feed on *The Radicalisation of Bradley Manning* live streaming website allows the audience to communicate with one another (and with the administrator and the technician of the streaming) and respond to the performance in real time. The use of the Internet in NTW assists relationships between the local and the global (which is of increasing concern to community-based theatre) and between theatre and non-theatre communities to be developed.

I also examine global radical democracy within the context of interculturalism, looking at cyberformance as a site for global participation and conflictual discourses. In Verhoeven's *Life Streaming* (2010) and Rimini Protokoll's *Call Cutta in a Box* (2008–13), performers are located in different cities from the audience, connecting Sri Lanka with London and Calcutta with Berlin, respectively. Despite the geographical distance, audience members share moments of real contact and intimacy with the performers. In *Life Streaming*, the spectators experience the suffocating atmosphere of Sri Lanka when warm water floods the performance space at the end of the show. In *Call Cutta in a Box*, performers in India manipulate the performance space in Berlin enhancing the sense of Dixon's 'virtual touch' (2006, p. 70). The cultural differences between performers and audience members also allow established cultural bias to be challenged and audience sensitivity to be aroused on key topics related to the performers' community. I refer to Annie Abrahams' *Angry Women* (2011–12) and Øystein Ulsberg Brager's Skype production, *You Are Invited* (2011), to discuss remote collaboration between artists from different cultures who co-create online work without necessarily having met face-to-face. In Abrahams' multilingual performance, female artists talk about their anger in their mother tongue, whereas *You Are Invited*

DOI: 10.1057/9781137577047.0006

presents a variety of one-to-one Skype mini-shows creating babelic cyberformances for international audiences.

The chapter concludes with a discussion on local and global cyber-formance exchanges, analysing the use of the cyberstage as a public and private space for street and domestic cyberformances. I investigate the Internet as an archival space in the case of the Høyblokka Project, where Trondheim citizens' memories of the city's old hospital and the project's site-specific performance are documented and stored on the virtual replica of the demolished building, through Derrida's notion of archivization. I also discuss the capacity of the Internet to expand public participation and community engagement. The similarity between musicians Merton and Ben Fold and their Chatroulette-based cyber-street theatres reveal the problem of virtual visualization of the Internet and raise ethical considerations and copyright concerns. Merton stages one-to-one music interactions with random online audiences, whereas Fold conducts concerts in which online audience members become performers for offline ones and vice versa. Further, I examine the Internet as a space for creative activism through Jamieson's and Field Broadcast's eco-theatre and workshops and Waterwheel's interactive 'water-themed' platform to conclude that cyberformance offers a new space for community participation and artist–activist collaboration where one does not have to choose between politics and art. For example, Jamieson, in collaboration with other artists, uses private and public spaces to bring offline and online communities together on UpStage to foster radical democracy, while Field Broadcast makes windows pop up unexpectedly on audience computer screens during live streaming. Thus, the Internet is evidenced as a successful tool for community-engaging and participatory theatre, providing pluralistic spaces for radical participation and engagement through critical interaction.

## 2.1   Towards a democratic theatre: the 'radicalization' of National Theatre Wales

The term radicalization tends to convey a negative meaning, as it has been connected with theories of extremism and is used to describe terrorism or other forms of socio-political or religious violence (O'Loughlin, Boudeau and Hoskins, 2011; Schmid, 2013) and a kind of pedagogy and practice (Kershaw, 1999; Cohen-Cruz, 1998). Despite this, however, I

DOI: 10.1057/9781137577047.0006

use the term here to reclaim its positive side as a constructive differentiation from the traditional, a new suggestion and a progression from established knowledge or truth. I also attempt to connect it to Mouffe's agonistic project of 'radical and plural democracy' (1996, p. 134), which aims towards the equality and liberty of a wider range of social relations and participation: 'Radical politics should concern "life" issues and be "generative", allowing people and groups to make things happen; and democracy should be envisaged in the form of a "dialogue", controversial issues being resolved through listening to each other. There is much talk nowadays of a "democratization of democracy"' (quoted in Laclau and Mouffe, 1985, p. xv).

Radical democracy is understood as the type of participatory democracy that allows the coexistence and clash of different interpretations – 'agonistic pluralism' (Jezierska, 2011, p. 25) – which, according to Mouffe, is always linked to 'conflict' (1996, p. 138). As Miessen argues, any form of participation is already a form of conflict: 'In order to participate in any environment or given situation, one needs to understand the forces of conflict that act upon that environment' (2010, p. 53). Both Mouffe and Miessen define participation as a dialogical form of critical engagement, as opposed to 'pseudo-participation', 'a proposition to let others contribute to the decision-making process' (Miessen, 2010, p. 14). In agreement with this definition, *participation* in this book refers to Miessen's (2010) *conflictual participation* rather than to *pseudo-participation* strategies, such as contemporary forms of representative democracy and referendum that provide ready-made solutions for participants to choose.

However, radical democracy is not that 'radical' at all. Instead, it is a contemporary re-interpretation of participative democracy of the Ancient Greek *polis-kratos* (city-state). Aristotle, in his *Poetics*, defined the democratic 'citizen'[1] 'as one who participates in giving judgement and holding office' (1981 [1962], p. 168). In contrast to contemporary society, the structure of communities in the different Ancient Greek *poleis* (cities) was too small for all citizens to participate in political debates and decisions held in the *agora* (Green, 1994, pp. 8–10). Apart from activities in the *agora*, theatre and drama also played a significant role in ancient Greek participatory democracy. To be an audience member in Ancient Athens was a fundamental political act, 'where to be in an audience is above all to play the role of [a] democratic citizen' (Goldhill, 1997, p. 54). As J. R. Green clarifies, '[d]ramatic performances were [...] put on by and for the community, and although foreigners were allowed to attend the

DOI: 10.1057/9781137577047.0006

Great Dionysia, they were not involved in the other festivals, and direct participation in any case remained an Athenian prerogative' (1994, p. 9).

Ancient Greek theatre allowed direct community engagement and interaction, as part of the role of the democratic citizen, mainly in the form of audience sounds of approval or disapproval – a kind of a democratically elected repertoire. As Paul Cartledge notes, theatre in Ancient Greece was considered 'too important to be left solely to theatrical specialists' (1997, p. 3). Although outdoor theatre, such as Greek tragedy and *commedia dell'arte*, was interactive, the history of indoor theatre has mainly been a history of audience 'passivity' (Green, 1994, p. 9). However, contemporary forms of participatory art, such as immersive theatre and site-specific performances, return to more interactive performance strategies, 'to restore and realise a communal, collective space of shared social engagement' (Bishop, 2012, p. 275). Hence, here radicalization serves as a term to describe the re-democratization of theatre in terms of audience conflictual participation in interactive and participative theatre.

According to McGrath (2013) this interactive turn, which 'mirrors the opposite move a hundred years or so ago when theatre became more "flat", more screen-like', is influenced by the Internet generation. Although Mouffe describes the Internet as an 'autistic' form of radical democracy, 'where people are only listening to and speaking with people that agree with them' (quoted in Carpentier and Cammaerts, 2006, p. 6), according to Dahlberg and Siapera, many 'radical democrats' believe that the Internet provides space for 'radical democratic practice' (2007, p. 6): 'The internet is seen as providing space for the free flow of information, open debate of problems, and the formation of rational-critical public opinion, all of which enable citizen scrutiny of power and input into decision-making' (Dahlberg and Siapera, 2007, p. 3).

NTW, launched in November 2009 under the artistic direction of John E. McGrath, uses the Internet as a space to promote radical democracy and debate in theatre making and staging. It is one more example of the digitalization of national theatres in the United Kingdom, a digitalization that serves both the theatrical institution and its productions. Operating from a small base in Cardiff's city centre, just 152 miles away from NTLive, NTW has no permanent theatre building; instead, the nation of Wales is its stage. As noted on the company's website, NTW can be found 'around the corner, across the mountain and in your digital backyard', while previous productions have been held 'from forests to beaches, from aircraft hangars to post-industrial towns, village halls to nightclubs'

DOI: 10.1057/9781137577047.0006

(NTW, 2009–10). The site-specific approach of NTW marks the thresholds of the invisible borders of Wales, representing the community's issues, borders and boundaries in the NTW Assembly. In site-specific performance, 'it is the human traces on the landscape or in the urban maze that shape the scenario' (Kershaw, 2000, p. 127). According to Steve Blandford, national theatre institutions of newly devolved nations, namely Wales and Scotland, adopt such kinds of 'radical non-building-based models' that reflect the spirit of 'democratic engagement' of their old yet emerging national context and represent their national identity (2013, p. 12). As TV screens declared in a production of NTW, 'Wales is a radical country' (Williams, 2013). Indeed, NTW is the product of the power-shifts of the semi-detachment of Wales – 'Wales now has a semi-independent government with control over key services such as health, education, and culture' (McGrath, 2012, p. 1) – from the 'somewhat ironically titled "United Kingdom" ' (Blandford, 2013, p. 12), a detachment that allows the exploration of its own contexts and questions nationwide. As Blandford notes, '[t]he somewhat ironically titled "United Kingdom" does then present an opportunity to examine newly created small national contexts that are in close proximity and therefore constant dialogue with one another' (2013, p. 12).

NTW has a complex relationship with nation and identity. Its bilingual character, a relatively small population and the history of existing Welsh professional theatre led McGrath (2012) and the rest of the company to formulate an interactive vision and community-engagement mission:

> The specific time had some interesting features to it. 2009 was the point at which web 2.0 had really established itself and the prospect of building a genuine interactive online community was very real. And within theatre itself, the old divide between 'professional' and 'community' work (the traditional terms used in the UK) was breaking down as companies such as Punchdrunk popularized interactive theatre, and artists such as Rimini Protokoll created internationally renowned work with performers who had often never been on stage before. (McGrath, 2012, p. 2)

For that reason, NTW (2009–14) created the National Theatre Wales Community blog from the very beginning of its existence, a community site as an equivalent of a venue, 'a digital backyard', a space where artists, audience and activists can meet and talk, an interactive platform that allows the Welsh community to engage with and participate in the company's work, or, as McGrath (2013) suggests, 'a space of co-creation rather than just content publishing':

DOI: 10.1057/9781137577047.0006

I often describe the community as the equivalent of the cafe-bar area if we had a venue (which we don't) – the place where people talk about what they've seen, where artists meet to discuss future projects, where there are notices from all sorts of people on the notice board, and where you sometimes go by yourself in the hope of running into someone interesting. (McGrath, 2013)

Therefore, digital technology here serves as a theatre-building exercise rather than as a virtual extension of an existing platform such as NTLive or *Quizoola24!*. Although the blog focuses on theatre and arts, McGrath (2013) rightly points out that 'there is certainly a political element', evident in the strong presence of Welsh community issues in the blog, as local issues are debated in NTW productions. However, the online presence of NTW crosses the geographical barriers of Wales, extending from the national and the local to the global. The blog, for instance, began a petition about the Freedom Theatre in Palestine, which was then sent to the Israeli Embassy (McGrath, 2013). As Mouffe argues, 'the global is always locally constituted and vice versa' and, thus, should not be considered as opposed scales (quoted in Miessen, 2010, p. 150). NTW productions also look at the relationship between the local and the global, as discussed later in this section.

In contrast to Forced Entertainment's controlled interaction with the audience and the restricted, professional seriousness of the NTLive website, the community of Wales controls the content of the NTW blog: 'anyone can post their events now, not just NTW' (McGrath, 2013). In response to being asked how they control content on the site, McGrath (2012) stated, 'we trust our community to regulate itself'. McGrath and the NTW Assembly use the blog as a place to find inspiration for their projects. As a result, the NTW Assembly programme runs 'democratically-elected creative arts projects' (NTW, 2010a), through public discussion and online voting, to extend the role of the public in decision making.

We are hoping to build on that project over the coming years, to a large-scale project based in a place and on a theme voted on by the public online. I think it's a very interesting development. However, I don't think we will ever go down the route of people just electing the repertoire online – that feels too simplistic. (McGrath, 2013)

According to social media specialist Tom Beardshaw (2012), the NTW blog moves beyond social media basics and tackles the issue of younger generation engagement in the theatre community 'by giving them a

DOI: 10.1057/9781137577047.0006

public voice in the theatre community, and encouraging them to use it'. As the Internet is popular among the younger generation, cyberformance can be used as a tactic to attract young audiences, as discussed in the case of *Such Tweet Sorrow*. However, for this same reason, cyberformance has been wrongly accused of marginalizing older audiences unfamiliar with the world of computers. Although basic knowledge of computer and Internet use is essential, cyberformance is not a genre created merely by the young artist for the young audience. People of all ages who have access to the Internet can participate in online theatre projects.

Apart from the community blog, from its inception NTW has used Internet technology in many different ways in actual artistic productions. For instance, in the production of Gary Owen's *Love Steals Us from Loneliness* (NTW, 2010b), set in his hometown of Bridgend, the company created an online interactive map to collect 'experiences, thoughts and opinions from places in Bridgend'. By the end of its launch year, NTW attracted the interest of community bloggers, who during an event for the Port Talbot community – Michael Sheen's *The Passion* – 'updated audiences beyond Port Talbot via a designated online world at port-talbot.com' (NTW, 2011). The project, according to McGrath (2013), had a definite political impact on the audience.

In April 2012, a total of 8,804 people (including the author) across 76 countries watched the online live stream of *The Radicalisation of Bradley Manning* (NTW, 2012), Tim Price's 'contemporary Welsh political drama' (McGrath, 2013), which opened at Tasker Milward School in Haverfordwest – the school where Bradley Manning completed his secondary education – and continued its tour in different schools of the country (NTW, 2012). I watched the live feed of the show on 27 April 2012, staged at Connah's Quay High School in Flintshire, UK. Despite the distributed audience being fewer than during NTLive's *Phèdre* broadcast, the low-definition streaming and other technical issues – the four-camera live feed was pushed up through an iPhone because the Internet speed dropped during the performance – the *Bradley Manning* experiment gave a strong sense of audience co-presence similar to the #quizoola24 online audience Twitter communication. Apart from the chat box that the audience used mainly to discuss technical issues with the administrator and the technician, the real-time Twitter feed of #NTW18 was available for website users to read. As Charlotte Runcie (2013) wrote in a review of the production, '[p]erformances are streamed online with social media debates encouraged, which does a lot to highlight the strength of biographical theatre over blockbuster biopic: the show has evolved to include updates from Manning's trial as it happens, while the internet responds to the performance in real time'.

Alongside the live stream, the dedicated website that hosted the project offered further information about the themes and events mentioned in the play as well as a chat function for the online audience, 'so that there would be a debate at the heart of every performance' (McGrath, 2013). According to McGrath (2013), the production allowed NTW to develop the relationship between the local and the global. This is entirely consistent with the increasing concerns of community-based performances that combine the local with the global (Govan, Nicholson and Normington, 2007), a fact corroborated in Rose de Wend Fenton and Lucy Neal's statement, '[t]he paradox is that often the more personal or intimate the story is, the more universally it is understood' (2005, p. 73). However, as Ball (2013) argues, *The Radicalisation of Bradley Manning* 'didn't just extend the reach of the production, but built a new community of interest, dialogue and depth of understanding around it by accessing people through networks who were not necessarily interested in theatre, but in freedom of expression and Wikileaks'.

Where NTLive is thinking big, NTW is thinking equally adventurously small. NTW offers a model of democratically elected (through public and online discussion, sharing and exchange) and universally distributed theatre. The radicalization and re-localization of NTW allowed citizens of Wales to reclaim theatre as a public good, while the relationship between the local and the global encouraged interactions between different communities and cultures.

## 2.2    Intermedial interculturalism: *Life Streaming* and *Call Cutta in a Box*

The Internet provides dialogical spaces for people to connect, communicate and share, in the context of radical democracy. Clay Shirky clearly distinguishes conversation from sharing information, arguing that online conversation in any format – via email, text messages or other media – 'creates more of a sense of community [to online users] than sharing' (2008, p. 50). However, sharing the same online platform allows conversation mechanisms to work. The Internet provides a meeting point for cultures and, as John Martin states, 'at meeting points there is always some sort of exchange' (2004, p. 1). According to Josette Feral, despite geographical distances 'the questions are the same everywhere' (1996, p. 55); the answers are what differ. This section looks at the use of the Internet for intercultural exchange, investigating how interculturalism manifests itself in cyberformance.

> Interculturalism is an urgent topic in the twenty-first century. As cities and nations move beyond the monochromatic, as human traffic between nations and cultures (both willing and unwilling) increases, as hybridity and syncretism (the merging of forms) become increasingly characteristic of cultural production everywhere, and as nineteenth-century nationalism gives way to twenty-first century *trans*nationalism, it becomes imperative that the ways in which cultural exchange is performed be critically re-examined. (Knowles, 2010, p. 3; emphasis in the original)

I use the term interculturalism to imply a positive form of globalization of conflict (in terms of radical democracy), where cultural exchange is taking place, and as a political phenomenon, 'towards a larger sense of the membership of the world as a whole' (Rebellato, 2009, p. 6) in the Internet age. In particular, I examine cyberformance as a site for global participation and conflictual discourses.

Considering the aforementioned blackout during political uprisings, it would be naive to believe that the Internet is democratically distributed. Despite the democratic potentials and practices of the Internet, its use is inextricably linked to the regime of each country and its level of freedom of expression. Theatre, 'as a medium for creating a shared language of the imagination that can cross cultural barriers' (De Wend Fenton and Neal, 2005, p. 73), can cover this communication gap, connecting distant geographical and cultural places using the Internet in combination with theatrical means, acknowledging the political significance of intercultural dialogue in intermedial performance. As Martin asserts, '[w]e now live in a world where people of different cultures and ethnicities meet and mix freely, creating a dynamic space for re-assessment of our identities, and opportunities for our performing arts to be enriched and to reflect the societies in which we live' (2004, p. 1).

For the production of *Life Streaming*, Verhoeven (2010) installed antennas in Sri Lanka – the country has no 'fast' Internet as the Western world is used to – to connect distant people to share experiences. The project, performed as part of the 2010 LIFT, was a one-to-one, online performance experience. Each member of the audience in London 'chatted' with a member of the troupe located on a beach 8,000 kilometres away,

DOI: 10.1057/9781137577047.0006

through an application similar to Skype. The premiere of the show was postponed because a tornado in Sri Lanka threw off the antenna from a roof. Apart from technical problems, Verhoeven (2012) also had to overcome issues of difference in cultural background and language. Breaking geographical, technical and cultural barriers, *Life Streaming* commented on the media presentation of individuals as passive victims, focusing on the case of the 2004 tsunami in Indonesia: 'In *Life Streaming* there was a "hidden agenda" that became [ ... ] the heart of the piece. ([Verhoeven] wanted to let the spectator think about the manipulation he/she might have gone through in the piece, and is going through in his/her daily life when he/she sees disaster aid marketing.)' (Verhoeven, 2012).

Challenging established cultural bias, Verhoeven manipulated the audience to teach a lesson about media manipulation. *Life Streaming* was my first experience of online theatre; I was a member of the audience in London. A performer from Sri Lanka asked whether I had lost *something* important lately, and I immediately thought of *someone* important; my mind raced to death, expecting to hear a tragic story of loss from the other side of the computer, when, surprisingly, the performer told me that he misplaced his stuff everyday and that he had lost his watch lately. It was a pleasant shock to realize that life continues after disasters.

Before entering the specially built Internet cafe van outside the Royal National Theatre (see Verhoeven, 2010), next to the Thames River, we were asked to leave our shoes and our personal belongings with the performance team. Each participant audience member then sat in front of a computer, while Verhoeven gave guidelines and set conventions, preparing us for technical failures during the performance. The computer screen was the empty, blank stage that gradually filled with worlds, Google maps, images, videos and sounds. The performers and the audience wrote the performance script as the show progressed on the empty screen.

Verhoeven (2012) does not use scenography to indicate or suggest a location: 'As a scenographer I wanted to start with an empty stage many times. I liked the idea that images appear on the moment a thought pops up in your head.' Cyberformance provides creative tools for new experimentations in scenography by mixing pre-recorded and real-time forms, such as real-time text writing and drawing, against the boundaries of gravity and physicality, as studied mainly by the 'magic' stage of Artaud's (1958 [1938]) theatre and its double. Examples of these tools include set and costume designs of SL avatars (e.g., Elif Ayiter's costume shop on SL)

DOI: 10.1057/9781137577047.0006

and Richard Beacham's Theatron Project (see King's Visualisation Lab, 1999). Further study about scenography in cyberformance is needed to address its role in more detail.

Although the whole *Life Streaming* performance was set up on the cyberstage, the ending brought the audience back to the physical space: warm water flooded the van in London as performers, 8,000 kilometres away in Sri Lanka, ran towards the sea. For both parties, this real-time experience created a feeling of being in the same *spaceless* place at the same time and sharing the same experience, despite the *bodyless* state. The water, the rain and the suffocating atmosphere penetrated the online environment through touch, smell and sound. The use of physical elements created the sense of co-presence and co-experience, similar to virtual three-dimensional environments, thus connecting the two distant geographical spaces. This is a great example of what Dixon calls 'virtual touch' (2006, p. 70), a moment of real contact and intimacy between physical and virtual bodies and physical and virtual spaces. Verhoeven's (2010) use of the Internet in his *Life Streaming* production intended to directly involve the spectators in the performance and create personal contact between the 20 local performers and the global audience. In fact, the audience grew so attached to the performers and their stories that most of them continued to send the performers messages.

The internationally known theatre company Rimini Protokoll (started in 2000 by Helgard Haug, Stefan Kaegi and Daniel Wetzel) has also regarded the Internet as a tool for intercultural communication – 'an area of interaction where new forms are created' (Martin, 2004, p. 2) – using physical elements as a strategy to connect distant cities. In contrast to Verhoeven's project, Rimini Protokoll's *Call Cutta in a Box* (2008–13) used existing, established technology that had made India 'become the back office of the western world' (Haug, 2012). The Internet featured as a vital tool for socio-political criticism and for arousing audience sensitivity on the topic. Call centres are intercultural communication hubs, where people are constantly sharing exclusive moments of exchange, without meeting the person on the other side of the phone line. *Call Cutta in a Box* discussed the notion of distance and proximity in such types of sound communications, by creating the opportunity to see/meet the person behind the voice at either end of the line, using theatre as 'the betwixt-and-between of peoples at the centre of the barter' (Kershaw, 2000, p. 127).

The first version of the production, called *Call Cutta* (2005), was a guided walk; selected young Indians with communications skills 'guid[ed] people in Kolkata (first) and then in Berlin through streets and lanes to secret places and finally to a shop window, where for a moment they could see one another through a technology – not Skype yet, similar but very slow' (Haug, 2012). In 2008, however, for the indoor one-to-one *Call Cutta in a Box* version, the company explored in more depth the interactive potentials of the Internet, experimenting with tools that allowed the performers in India to reach and manipulate things in the performance space in Berlin, such as switch on the light, send a picture, open files in the computer and send sounds. Helgard Haug (2012) described the 2008 performance as follows:

> The phone will be ringing when you are opening the door and a person on the other end of the line will know your name and ask you when he/she can prepare a cup of tea for you. If you agree the kettle in the office will be switched on and an hour of a conversation between a person in a call center in India and you will start.

Thus, *Call Cutta in a Box* challenged the boundaries of *virtual touch* by developing a degree of intimacy and interaction between performers and participant audience members and between the distributed spaces in which the performance took place (see discussion in Chapter 1; see also Dixon, 2006, p. 70).

According to Haug (2012), many similarities can be found between online theatre and conventional theatre. For instance, in *Call Cutta in a Box*,

> the callers had to slip in[to] roles, had to pretend being someone else, get an English or American name (according to the market they were serving Shuktara became for example Sandy), pretend to be in the direct neighborhood by knowing the results of the recent football or soccer-game and chat on the weather and when they made a deal, the other callers were giving applause. (Haug, 2012)

However, Haug (2012) does argue that it is difficult to concentrate in the Internet space and that online directing makes sense only if the remote collaborators know each other in the old fashioned, face-to-face way.

Conversely, Abrahams (2011b), biologist and performance artist, collaborated with up to 24 women of different nationalities, whom she met through the Internet, without any personal or direct connection, and whose work was related to contemporary art practices and computer-based performances, for her *Angry Women* (2011–12) webcam performance (see Abrahams, 2011–12). As Abrahams (2012) explains, 'I

DOI: 10.1057/9781137577047.0006

considered my work partly as performance [in 1996] – in that space of public solitude. I still like to see all my activities (also writing, teaching etc.) as performance; my online work is that too.' *Angry Women* is a remote communication and collaboration research project that looks at female anger as a pretext. The project was originally started for Abrahams' show *Training for a Better World*, at the Centre Régional D'Art Contemporain Languedoc-Roussillon (2011–12) in France. All artists sat in front of their own computer in their own country during the performance. They were asked to talk about their anger in their mother tongue. The aim of the project was to reveal moments that human beings cannot control them-selves and to perform those (emotional) moments that people usually prefer not to show. Although the performance was based on frames, there was no specific format or idea for the performance outcome (Abrahams, 2011a). *Angry Women* has been performed online and in a mixed online–offline format. The show was exhibited live and was recorded in several galleries, including at London's Furtherfield Gallery; it was also part of the 121212 UpStage Festival. According to Abrahams (2012), her work is a 'hybrid thing with aspects from fine art, theater, but also film, poetry and even science'.

An alternative example of remote collaboration is the Skype performance *You Are Invited* (2011) by Imploding Fictions, a Norway-based theatre company founded by Philip Thorne and Øystein Ulsberg Brager (see Imploding Fictions, 2011, 2014). In 2010, Paul Osuch, founder and artistic director of the Anywhere Theatre Festival,[2] invited the company to participate in the festival in Brisbane, Australia (Brager, 2012). However, owing to a lack of funds, the company decided to collaborate with colleagues spread across the globe and devise a performance using Skype as a theatrical stage. *You Are Invited* consisted of five mini-shows performed from five different countries/places: Norway, United States (Texas), Spain, Germany and England. The show was accessed by calling the Skype account 'youareinvitedentry', where Brager explained to the audience how the show works and gave the next Skype account name to call to continue the performance; a new account name/number was given at the end of each performance to move onto the next mini-show. The Internet was used here both as a tool and as a space. According to Brager (2012), 'it was a tool to make collaborations happen that would otherwise not happen, but it is also a space in the sense that it is an arena where people meet. In our case: Audiences meeting performers.'

DOI: 10.1057/9781137577047.0006

The five groups/performers responded differently to the performance topic, breaking the logical sequence of the piece: 'only one of them interacted with the audience, the other performed what could be described as a live film' (Brager, 2012). Despite the one-to-one relationship between the audience and the performers, where the former had to call and be accepted by the latter, the mini-shows did not give opportunity for further participation and interaction, and so cannot be referred to as theatre. Although Michele White notes that the Internet/computer audience was 'much too close to the screen in order to enact a classic film viewing position' (2006, p. 77), it was close enough to enact a LiveTV viewing position.

Notwithstanding the structural similarities of *Life Streaming* and *Call Cutta in a Box*, there is a vital difference between the performances. Despite the one-to-one communication in the performances, the participant audience members in *Life Streaming* were all in the same space and shared the same experience as a group, whereas the participant audience members in *Call Cutta in a Box* received an individual experience in an empty room. In *Angry Women* and *You Are Invited*, participants had a more intimate relationship with the show as they could watch it from their private space using their personal computer. Furthermore, performers in *Life Streaming* and *Call Cutta in a Box* shared the same space during the performance, whereas performers in *Angry Women* and *You are Invited* enacted remotely. Analogous to the significance of the use, design and construction of the performance space (i.e., the proscenium and the auditorium) in conventional theatre, online platforms and offline spaces where performances are created and received are equally important in cyberformances. In *Life Streaming* and *Call Cutta in a Box*, the physical aesthetics of the performance space empowered the notion of co-presence and proximity in cyberformance. The intermedial use of the Internet turned the computer screen into an intercultural window, connecting distant people, cultures and places to redress the performative balance.

## 2.3   Towards a public theatre: cyber-street theatre, domestic theatre and activist theatre

The intermedial exchange between theatre and the Internet in cyberformance is responsible for the radicalization of both agencies in terms

DOI: 10.1057/9781137577047.0006

of democratization. The World Wide Web is a virtual world consisting of private and public platforms where local and global exchanges are taking place at a continuous, rapid pace. This section analyses the use of the cyberstage as public and private spaces, discussing cases of street and domestic cyberformances that aim to engage the public in theatre with the help of the Internet.

Høyblokka (2010–12), which means 'tower block' in Norwegian, is an art-based research project that started in early 2010 and investigates the nature of memories and remembering in site-specific performance. Akin to NTW's Bridgend memory map, the Høyblokka – Post Mortem Project focused on collecting memories from Trondheim citizens about their city's old hospital building that was demolished to make space for a new, modern hospital. The site-specific project used interactive media technology throughout its archiving process. The outcome was a live performance (on 30 January 2011) staged in front of the old city hospital in the middle of its demolition. The performance, thus, was an official funeral of the old hospital: 'Despite the cold weather more than one thousand citizens gathered at the ruins to take part in the ritual' (Høyblokka, 2010–12). Citizens of Trondheim played a crucial role in the Høyblokka Project, which could not have been accomplished without the active participation and engagement of the community.

Apart from the live performance, the research group created a virtual duplicate of the hospital in the project's online blog to keep its memory alive. Each window of the virtual building contains stories and memories related to the hospital in different forms, such as videos, pictures, texts and sounds. The use of the Internet as an archive in the Høyblokka blog demonstrates its ability to store different forms of data, forming memories of events, buildings and moments. Hence, the spaceless cyberspace can be considered as a memory space that mirrors moments of reality, a balance between 'the host and the ghost' of public spaces (Govan, Nicholson and Normington, 2007, p. 139). Although the hospital no longer exists, it has a strong virtual presence. The Høyblokka Project also reveals the power of the Internet in terms of expanding public participation, as the collection of such large amounts of information (in this case, personal memories) – as well as leading a 'potato revolution' (like in Greece) – would not be possible without the reach of the Internet.

Jacques Derrida addressed memory and the 'question of archives' in a lecture at a 1994 international colloquium in London: 'The technical structure of the *archiving* archive also determines the structure of the *archivable* content even in its very coming into existence and in its relationship to the future. The archivization produces as much as it records the event. This is also our political experience of the so-called news media' (Derrida, 1995, p. 17; emphasis in the original). Memory in the Internet age is primarily archival – the notion of memory as archive has been studied by Irving Velody (1998) – as recorded by different platforms such as blogs, Facebook and Twitter. Derrida's notion of archivization is central in the case of Høyblokka, where the blog provides access to the hospital's '[memory] archive, its constitution and its interpretation' (Derrida, 1995, p. 4).

Another example of cyber-street theatre is 'Mertonian Chatroulette'. Merton (2014) is an improvisation piano player who gained media attention during 2010 for his YouTube videos of music interactions with random people he met on Chatroulette.[3] His solo performances surprised the random interlocutors, who became audience members for his one-to-one live improvisations and performers for his recorded videos on YouTube. Unlike in the Høyblokka Project, where participants were invited to take active part and share their memories, Merton's audience got involved unexpectedly. Similarly to street theatre, Merton needed to hold the interest of the random audience, who could leave the session at any time by clicking the 'next' button (available at: http://www.youtube.com/watch?v=JTwJetox_tU). Mertonian Chatroulette's use of the Internet as a public space can thus be considered as a form of cyber-street theatre, what Sue-Ellen Case describes as 'a new kind of street theater in the cybersphere, erupting in social spaces where people pass through or hang out' (2007, p. 31). Furthermore, while Merton used the Internet as a space for site-specific performance, Høyblokka's site functioned just as 'archive space'.

Merton did not use his real name and, because of similarities in appearance, a considerable number of people believed him to be musician Ben Folds. Folds, in turn, used the Mertonian Chatroulette technique in his concerts, which he uploaded on YouTube under the name *Ode to Merton*. The *Ode to Merton* developed Merton's technique on stage, with offline audiences observing and actively reacting in the live composition of Folds' improvisational songs. A combination of indoor and outdoor theatre was created, where offline audience members became performers for online ones and online participants performed for offline audiences. The YouTube concerts empowered the audience's belief that Folds is Merton, which led to them appearing together in a YouTube video to prove

DOI: 10.1057/9781137577047.0006

they are not the same person (available at: http://www.youtube.com/ watch?v=BWGXVhBW9SA). This raises ethical considerations and copyright questions in relation to online performance and reveals the problem of virtual visualization. In the bodyless cyberspace, characteristics such as a person's height, body shape and facial details are lost, making it difficult for someone to visualize exactly how a person really looks.

In addition to the random form of participation in Mertonian Chatroulette and the call for participation in the Høyblokka Project, the audience invited performers in Jamieson and Paula Crutchlow's *make-shift* (2010–12) to perform in their private houses. The *make-shift* presentation is a networked performance about recycling which approaches, interactively, the subject of political responsibilities of peoples' daily actions that transform the world we live in (see *make-shift*, 2010–14). The 'on-site' and online participants created kites using their recyclable rubbish, while a discussion on pollution on the earth was taking place on UpStage. Jamieson used the term 'on-site' or 'proximal' to describe an audience who exists together in a physical space (where the performance takes place), in contrast to an 'online', distributed audience (2008, p. 35).

Staged on UpStage, *make-shift* required a commercial streaming company for the live audiovisual streaming of the two locations of the performance simultaneously. Jamieson and Crutchlow, situated in their respective houses, led the performance for the on-site audience, connected through a specially designed online interface. This gave the online audience the opportunity to follow the events in both houses and enter the private spaces of the on-site audience; concomitantly, it allowed the on-site audience to follow both the online audience discussion through a chat box and the on-site audience in the second location by using a projector. The triangular relationship built on the UpStage stage allowed space for further interpretation and discussion.

However, *make-shift*'s focus on on-site audience members created a distance from online ones, who were mainly beholders of, rather than participants in, the performance. Despite the physical distance, all online audience members were part of the same team, sharing technical problems as well as information related to the performance and the weather forecasts. They even informed each other every time they managed to reconnect on UpStage due to technical problems. This meeting of audience members from different locations and time zones in the spaceless

DOI: 10.1057/9781137577047.0006

cyberspace to discuss everyday issues is in itself a very powerful element of cyberstage's socio-political space.

Jamieson (with Martin Eisenbarth) also used the aesthetics of ecology in her collaboration with four organizations (Furtherfield, London, UK; APO33, Nantes, France; MAD Emergent Art Centre, Eindhoven, The Netherlands; and Schaumbad Freies Atelierhaus, Graz, Austria) for the cyberformance project *We Have a Situation!* (2012–13), which is 'a series of live, trans-border, online–offline participatory performances addressing current cross-cultural European [eco-]issues' (see WeHaveASituation, 2013). The *We Have a Situation!* Project collaborators visited galleries, laboratories and libraries across Europe to lead workshops, discussions and performances about cyberformance, each time focusing on a different eco-issue (chosen by the local participants): e-waste was researched in the *London Situation* (19–23 March 2013), Boeing plane recycling in the *Nantes Situation* (9–12 April 2013), global mobility in the *Eindhoven Situation* (15–18 April 2013) and Unidentified Flying Food (UFF) in the *Graz Situation* (17–22 May 2013). All workshop participants somehow got involved from before the workshops actually began, from helping decide the theme to the final performance to follow-up discussions, 'fostering active citizenship through creative networked collaboration' (European Cultural Foundation, 2013, p. 1). Participants from different countries connected online for the final performance discussion, and some got involved in the actual show, such as in the *London Situation* where participants (including the author) performed from Furtherfield Gallery.

The topic of ecology is of great interest among the cyberformance community. Like Jamieson's ecological focus in her two most recent works, intermedia artist Suzon Fuks too explores the theme of water through Waterwheel's interactive platform, launched in 2011. Fuks (2011) describes it as 'an online space where you can interact, share, perform and debate about water as a topic and metaphor, with people round the world or right next door.' The Waterwheel enhanced the potential of known cyberformance platforms by providing an online venue, the Tap, which is able to host up to six webcams simultaneously live streaming and offers tools for real-time interaction, such as volume change and image flip, hide, move, rotate, resize, delete, fade in or out and bring forward or take backwards while streaming. The Tap also contains drawing, audio, video, animation and slideshow tools as well as chat boxes to enable interaction between audiences and performers. Although Waterwheel is an open

DOI: 10.1057/9781137577047.0006

platform with immense possibilities, Fuks restricts its use by requesting that only performances and presentations in relation to water as a topic and metaphor be staged (Waterwheel Tap, 2011; Fuks, 2011). Water is inextricably connected with the Internet and its language. 'Surfing', for instance, in web language means to browse or move from site to site. Both the Internet and water serve here as a metaphor for eco-theatre.

Another online art platform that plays with the idea of nature is Field Broadcast (2010). Artists Rebecca Birch and Rob Smith run Field Broadcast, a project that provides downloadable applications from which broadcasts can be received live and unexpectedly on audiences' computer screens. The project examines 'the simultaneous experience of remoteness and proximity through live broadcasting' (Near Now, 2010–14). Although audience members download the application knowing its purpose and with the willingness to participate in the event, Field Broadcast works as a computer virus as a result of its unexpected character: when an artist makes a live broadcast, a loud 'ping' sound is heard and a window pops up on the screen. Hence, the experience – or even the 'non-experience' – of the live performance depends on the place and the situation the audience member is in at the moment of the live broadcast. Field Broadcast produced its first series of performances in collaboration with the Wysing Arts Centre in 2010. The performance series, also titled *Field Broadcast*, showcased the works of 33 artists who broadcast live their work from different UK-based landscapes (fields) for a period of nine days (8–16 May 2010). The artists used simple, available technology, such as video cameras, laptops and 3G mobile Internet connections, for streaming the unexpected live performances, shot in the fields.

According to Tiziana Terranova, '[f]ar from being an "unreal" empty space, the Internet is animated by cultural and technical labor through and through, a continuous production of value that is completely immanent to the flows of the network society at large' (2000, pp. 33–34). The interest of this 'network society' of cyberformers in ecology is part of the ongoing interest in community and activist theatre – what Bishop (2006) calls 'the social turn' – and is indicative of the increasing use of the Internet as a tool and space for participation. Kershaw has argued that participatory forms of performance, such as immersive theatre, 'are most likely to lead to new ecological forms of performance' (2000, p. 124) or art. Christopher Jury states that 'art, by definition and praxis (in a world determined by market forces), excludes the artist from the

DOI: 10.1057/9781137577047.0006

functional aspiration of bringing about political change', dismissing the very existence of 'political art' (2012, p. 5). However, Jury argues, 'creative activism' – the kind of activism that uses creative tools such as music, poetry, graphics, street theatre and other cultural objects to contribute to social, political and economic campaigns or movements – can replace the work of 'political artists', who focus on 'aesthetic legitimacy' questions instead of public discourse (2012, p. 5). Bishop (2006) likewise recognizes the issue of aesthetic legitimacy, opposing the political and the artistic aspects of community theatre in her article 'The social turn: collaboration and its discontents'. However, I believe cyberformance offers a new space for community and civil engagement and artist/activist collaboration, a space 'beyond these binary problematics' (Abrahams, 2011b) where one does not have to choose between politics and art. This is supported by Dixon's view that, in cyberspace, 'the personal is political' (2007, p. 463) and the view of web and installation artist Shu Lea Cheang that 'community' is 'what the Net is mostly about' (quoted in Dixon, 2007, p. 463).

The different examples studied in this chapter frame the participatory character of cyberformance in terms of community engagement. In the case of NTW, the Internet turned into an online cafe–bar area for public discussion and participation, promoting citizens' democratic engagement in terms of radical democracy. In cyberformance, local and global exchanges are taking place at a continuous, rapid pace, turning cyberstages into in-between platforms for intercultural exchange. Both *Live Streaming* and *Call Cutta in a Box* challenged the boundaries of these platforms, creating physical connections between geographically distant spaces. These differences are located between performers and audiences, as in the case of *Life Streaming* and *Call Cutta in a Box*, or between performers themselves, as seen in *Angry Women* and *You Are Invited*. The ability of cyberformance to break geographical and economic boundaries finds application in artists' remote collaborations, as discussed in the works of Abrahams and Brager. Using online and offline spaces, and public and private cyberstages, artists and researchers engage audiences in performance making and staging. The Høyblokka Project invited Trondheim citizens to share their memories using the Internet as a space for archivization, collecting individual and public memory; Merton surprised random Chatroulette users with his cyberstreet theatre in a similar way as Field Broadcast 'infected' the computer screen of audience members with UK-based landscapes. Finally, this

DOI: 10.1057/9781137577047.0006

chapter discussed the ecological and activist character of cyberformance through Jamieson's work to conclude that community is indeed what the Internet is mostly about.

The online participative theatre performances discussed in this chapter took place alongside the practical explorations of the Etheatre Project, inspiring my work as a cyberformance director and researcher. The performances influenced the project's experiments that explore the dialectical character of cyberformance for real-time political engagement and participation. In Chapter 3, I look at the chat box as a tool for radical democracy to achieve plurality and diversity in audience responses during a performance and to connect the local with the global in a similar way as NTW uses its blog. Interculturalism is also a key aspect of the Etheatre Project as different cultures are brought into discussion. In the *Cyberian Chalk Circle* (2011) production, Greek performers examine a political situation in the Middle East, through a cyber-New Zealand site, communicating in English with an international audience. Moreover, in the same way as Abrahams connects multilingual performers, I use remote collaboration in the *Etheatre Project and Collaborators* (2014) production to connect distant artists and create a collective performance about migration. The archival and activist character of the Internet is explored through *Merry Crisis and a Happy New Fear* (2012), a real-time verbatim performance in which public memories about the 2008 Greek riots, collected through an online questionnaire, create a protest cyberformance where real-time audience responses are archived in the chat box and incorporated into the script during the performance. I also use the viral strategies of Field Broadcast, 'infecting' the computer screens of audience members via the UpStage reset button devised to automatically reload all browsers connected to the platform, to demonstrate co-presence on the cyberstage and arouse audience sensitivity on political topics through the so-called virtual touch.

## Notes

1   Women, children and slaves were not considered 'citizens' in Ancient Athens.
2   The concept of the Brisbane-based Anywhere Theatre Festival is a performing theatre in non-theatre spaces, emerging as a response to the lack of theatre spaces in Brisbane (Anywhere, 2013).

DOI: 10.1057/9781137577047.0006

3   Its website describes Chatroulette as 'a place where you can interact with new people over text-chat, webcam and mic' (Chatroulette, 2009). The website pairs strangers from around the world for webcam-based conversations. This has become the meeting point for many offensive users, who present abusive images, which resulted in the bad reputation of the website.

DOI: 10.1057/9781137577047.0006

# 3
# The Etheatre Project: The Director as Discussion Facilitator

**Abstract:**. *Papagiannouli looks at the forms of cyber-adaptation, cyber-ethnotheatre and cyber-collaboration as directing methodologies for producing dialectical forms of political cyberformances (in Brechtian terms), with reference to the productions of* Cyberian Chalk Circle *(2011),* Merry Crisis and a Happy New Fear *(2012) and* Etheatre Project and Collaborators *(2014), respectively. The chapter also discusses the specific directorial work that was undertaken for each production to generate new knowledge in relation to directing political cyberformance. Audience participation is noted as retaining a key role in the making and staging of a cyberformance, where participants can co-direct, interact with the performance and become part of the collective ensemble of a company.*

Papagiannouli, Christina. *Political Cyberformance: The Etheatre Project*. Basingstoke: Palgrave Macmillan, 2016. DOI: 10.1057/ 9781137577047.0007.

The chapter discusses the directing methodologies of the Etheatre Project using Brecht's theories in order to study the role of the director as 'discussion facilitator' in political cyberformance. The term political cyberfomance is used here to describe directorial practices of *making cyberformance politically* (in Brechtian political theatre terms), rather than cyberformance with political content (see Barnett, 2015, p. 32). The political character of the Etheatre Project lies in the conflictual/dialectical participation of the audience in real time during the performance. In political cyberformance, the role of the director is to promote real-time discussion between audience members and performers in a chat box and assist the dialectical participation of spectators in the performance. In particular, I look at forms of cyber-adaptation, cyber-ethnotheatre and cyber-collaboration as directing methodologies for producing dialectical forms of political cyberformances, with reference to the productions of *Cyberian Chalk Circle* (2011), *Merry Crisis and a Happy New Fear* (2012) and *Etheatre Project and Collaborators* (2014), respectively. The chapter gives an outline of each production and discusses how the methodologies were developed during this research.

The final section examines strategies of co-presence embodiment that cyberformance mobilizes in the *in-between* space of the cyberstage, where everything is absent and present simultaneously. I study cyberformance conventions and their use to create the sense of co-presence in both the audience and the performers and to assist participation. The section reveals the importance of interactivity and audience participation in political cyberformance.

Brecht's directing methods were closely tied to his dialectical understanding of the world and, thus, contradiction was always a vital feature of his theatre (Mumford, 2009; Barnett, 2013). *Verfremdungeffekt* (V-effect), known as the alienation or more correctly as the distancing effect of epic theatre, was the main method Brecht used to dialectically politicize his performances; that is, 'to facilitate radical praxis' (Andrews, 2001, p. 2). Here, the familiar becomes the unfamiliar for critical observation to be empowered. Key Brechtian defamiliarization techniques include the anti-illusionism of breaking the fourth wall by making set changes visible (Bradley, 2006, p. 6; Mumford, 2009, p. 66; Andrews, 2011, p. 6); the 'fixing the not-but' strategy, that is, how alternative courses of action could have provoked different outcomes (Bradley, 2006, p. 5; Mumford,

DOI: 10.1057/9781137577047.0007

2009, pp. 66–67); and casting unsuitable actors for the character they acted out, such as young actors to play old characters (Mumford, 2009, p. 71). Non-realistic staging is essential for the critical 'distantification' of the spectator. As Barnett notes, '[r]ealism [ ... ] is something that applies to a given society as a whole because it reproduces the laws under which the dialectic works, regardless of apparent differences between individuals' (2011, p. 29), which substantiates that realism in Brecht is philosophical rather than aesthetic.

Brecht's theatre aimed to demonstrate social structures. To embody those structures and go beyond the individual, Brecht used *Gestus*, a form of stylized acting to demonstrate social class in relation to body language (Mumford, 2009, p. 54; Bradley, 2006, p. 6; Barnett, 2011, p. 29). *Gestus* is part of Brecht's 'paradoxical montage' technique, serving as a link between the original and interpretational text (Mueller, 1987; Doherty, 2000) – the so-called *fabel* (or *fabie*). To 'smash' the fourth wall and 'move beyond the superficial imitation of reality' (Barnett, 2011, p. 29), Brecht used collage and montage to create discontinuity and build a polymorphic space (Mueller, 1987; Doherty, 2000). On Brecht's polymorphic stage, large contradictions were exposed through the use of tableau aesthetics (Mueller, 1987), the 'to be and not to be' aspect of Brecht's distancing actor – the Brechtian double (Mitter, 1992) – as well as historicization ('H-effect') and adaptation, to distance the audience from the plot. Placing the performances into the past allowed the audience to review reality in relation to history, finding similarities and differences (Mitter, 1992, p. 35; Mumford, 2009). Brecht's work was to 'provoke' discussion, not to 'dominate' it (Barnett, 2013, p. 135).

As Jon Whitmore notes, 'theater cannot take place without the communication between the event and an audience', drawing attention to the fact that, as most theorists agree, 'spectators provide feedback to the performers and to one another' during a performance event (1994, p. 11). Mikhail Bakhtin has argued that 'any "social dialogue" of negotiation requires an audience [response]' to result in any meaningful change (quoted in Hutchison, 2005, p. 357; see also Bakhtin, 1981, p. 276). Brecht, likewise, evaluated his plays by observing the audience and critics' reactions during and after each performance and adapted his plays further keeping in mind audience response (Bradley, 2006, p. 1). Brecht's *Mother Courage and Her Children* (1939) is a well-known example of re-evaluation through audience observation, where Brecht made additions to the play to make 'Mother' less sympathetic to the audience after the play's 1941 'unsuccessful' production in Switzerland (Mayer, 1989). However, as Han Mayer (1989) argues, Brecht was dissatisfied with the audience's interpretation even after the changes. This was because although Brecht introduced the dialectical (distancing) 'spectating' (i.e., the 'act of being a spectator') with his theatre, he could not see that spectators' dialectical thinking was stronger than his own or than what he had expected. Indeed, in a classic theatrical experience the audience's interpretation cannot be clearly identified and analysed. Here, the participants' responses are hidden in the darkness of the third row.[1]

All these discussed strategies played a crucial role in the Etheatre Project, for the formation of both research and directing methodologies, in order to allow critical participation. In cyberformance, public discussion takes place in a text box; the use of the chat box gives space for the strong dialectical thinking of the spectators to be heard and for correlations with reality to be accomplished. Spectators become active participants in the communal space of the chat box, where writing serves as a way of thinking and as a communication tool. In the in-between space of the cyberstage, the chat box serves as a distancing tool where absence/presence and speech/writing – Derrida's oppositions of dominant notions of thinking (Reynolds, 2010) – coexist for the audience to communicate thoughts in real time and not after the performance as experienced in traditional theatre. Similarly to how Brecht aimed to dominate discussion during rehearsals, the work of the director in cyberformance is to facilitate discussion in real time during the performance.

I naturally employed a Brechtian approach in this research, recognizing the significance of Brechtian methodologies in my work so far as a theatre director. Similarly to how Brecht treated the classics and himself – 'if he found that [something] was opaque or boring, he cut it' (Weber, 2002, p. 85; see also Weber and Munk, 1967–68, p. 103; Subiotto, 1975, pp. 8, 110; Bradley, 2006, p. 12) – and to his elective use of Konstantin Stanislavsky's techniques of rehearsal (Mumford, 2009; Mitter, 1992), I too used his theories and practices selectively. For instance, I focused more on those theories that I found useful for my research and directing methods, such as the 'V-effect', and less on others that did not apply verbatim/precisely to the dialectical aesthetics of the Etheatre Project, such as the *Gestus*. The dialectical aesthetics of the Etheatre Project derive from text-based communication between performers and participants rather than on physical, body-oriented acting. Furthermore, despite the strong bond between Marxism and Brecht's political theatre – one of the main reasons for wrongly labelling Brecht as out-dated, especially as the present-day 'capitalist crisis' has renewed interest in Marxism (Wolff, 2010) – I do not focus on Marxism, but rather re-imagine the politics of Brecht for the age of the Internet. This chapter explores the prospects of forming political spaces through performance on cyberstage in relation to Brecht's political theatre directing methodologies and theories, questioning new forms of spatial relationships and dialectics. In particular, the epic theatre's distancing effect (V-effect) is reconsidered in relation to the bodyless, spaceless and liveness characteristics of cyberformance, focusing on the role of the dialectical 'spect-actor' drawing on Brechtian and Boalian readings.

In the Etheatre Project, I applied Brecht's dialectical and interactive approach to directing, using V-effect techniques to break the fourth wall and allow critical participation of the audience in the cyberformances. Despite my focus on Brecht's directorial work, I turn to Brecht in all of his roles – as a theatre and media theorist, director and author.

> [Brecht] really had almost a strangely split mind between the academic part of him that wrote theory and the man of the theatre who refused. He would, even in rehearsals, say 'I don't know what idiot wrote this theory, or what idiot wrote this part of the play', and it was a different Brecht. I think he is a landmark in theatre history, but like all landmarks, as one moves on, the landmark is behind. I don't think that today as a playwright and as a theorist one should take him either 100 per cent or zero, it's something naturally in between. (Brook, 1996, p. 52)

The in-betweeness of Brecht's personality, as suggested by Peter Brook (1996), provides an opportunity to develop new insights related to these polarities within the realm of Brecht's theories and practices in relation to digital technology. In particular, I study the application of Brechtian functions in cyberformance. A combination of the mentioned methodologies and digital tools results in a more democratic and interactive approach to theatre direction in terms of radical participation. Audience interaction is crucial for the dialectical, and thus political, character of cyberformance, which makes feasible Brecht's 'act of being a spectator'. According to Miessen, 'when participation becomes conflict, conflict becomes space', and 'political space entails the practice of decision-making, and judging' (2010, pp. 93, 249). Here, the Internet turns into a political, in-between space for real-time cyber-adaptation, cyber-ethnotheatre and cyber-collaboration, allowing participants' engagement in performance making and staging.

## 3.1   Cyber-adaptation: *Cyberian Chalk Circle*

The practical research of the Etheatre Project began with the preparation of a micro project called *Cyberian Chalk Circle* (2011), a production that aimed to pre-test the form of cyberformance. This first attempt of directing an online piece turned out to be the most important project within the Etheatre Project framework, in terms of audience political engagement and participation. *Cyberian Chalk Circle*, performed on 14 May (*CCC1*) and 11 November (*CCC2*) 2011 on UpStage and on 3 November 2012 on Waterwheel Tap (*CCC3*) by Evi Stamatiou (with the contribution of Prodromos Tsinikoris), was an online, interactive, chat-based adaptation of Brecht's *The Caucasian Chalk Circle* (1944).

To justify the use of the Internet as an essential tool in staging a theatre performance online, I began by looking for a Brechtian play or an individual scene that exemplified the absent present character, which is crucial for cyberformance to be staged on Skype or any other distancing communication tool. One of the first scenes that I came across was the famous 'stream scene' from *The Caucasian Chalk Circle*. In the original play, Grusha, a kitchen maid of the Caucasian palace, bids farewell to her fiancé Simon, who leaves to protect the governor during the palace revolution; Grusha, later on, finds and saves Michael, the governor's son. To raise Michael safely, Grusha gets married to a very ill man. One day, while she is washing linen by the stream, Simon arrives on the opposite bank. Grusha tries to explain to him what happened, but Simon leaves when she claims Michael is her child. In this stream scene, Simon and Grusha can see and talk to each other, but they cannot touch each other, which mirrors an online, distancing,

DOI: 10.1057/9781137577047.0007

network webcam conversation; Grusha's secret about Michael's identity creates the sense of a broken conversation, where one says something but means something else.

In *Cyberian Chalk Circle*, Grusha's story is placed in Egypt of 2011. While citizens of Cairo are removing their passwords from their WiFi routers so protesters can communicate with each other and the rest of the world, Grusha connects with the audience asking them to help her find Simon, an Egyptian soldier and her fiancé whom she lost because of the revolution. However, the audience do not have to merely find Simon; they also have to explain to him that Grusha got married (via an *urfi* contract) to someone else because she had found and kept a child, Michael. (In Egypt, women are not allowed to be single mothers; they must be married or have an *urfi* contract, a kind of a Muslim marriage.)

*Cyberian Chalk Circle* can thus be seen as an adaptation in two ways. First, as it derives from the title of Brecht's play, it indicates a transition from one medium to another: an intermedial exchange that entails the use of the Internet. Second, *Cyberian Chalk Circle* offers an alternative interpretation to the original text, because of the relocation of cultural, topical and temporal settings (Sanders, 2006, p. 19). To focus on the political character of the Etheatre Project, I am not going to discuss the form of intermedial adaptation (from one medium to another) as the topic has been much debated, especially in relation to adaptation from stage to cinema (Naremore, 2000; Cardwell, 2002; Leitch, 2005; Stam, 2005). Instead, I will focus on the idea of revisiting, reinterpreting and rethinking 'old' narratives in adaptation as interpretations of theatre direction. A 'transposition' of the original that, according to Linda Hutcheon, 'telling the same story from a different point of view [ ... ] create[s] a manifestly different interpretation' (2013, p. 8). I use *transposition* not to mean a shift either from one genre to another (from theatre to cyberformance) or from one medium to another (from theatre to the Internet) but rather as 'a change of frame and therefore context' (Hutcheon, 2013, p. 8). *Contextual adaptation* entails a major temporal, topical or cultural change of an original text. I thus lay emphasis on the distancing character of adaptation, which enforces a dialogical relationship between the old and the new narrative and between the real and mythical (*dialogism*), in terms of Brechtian political theatre directing methodologies. Although the form of contextual adaptation is a 'hot' topic, as transposition of a whole environment has been accused to 'reduce and simplify' the original play (Hutcheon,

2009, p. xi; MacArthur, Wilkinson and Zaiontz, 2009, p. xx), Brecht himself argued that 'directors should adopt a fresh approach towards the classics' (Bradley, 2006, p. 12).

The genre of adaptation is problematic per se, as adaptation charts a dialectical relationship with an original text. Neither Brecht nor Shakespeare, both ardent supporters of adaptation, got through critics accusations for adaptors' plagiarism and lack of originality (Beckley, 1962, p. 274). In the case of Shakespeare, stealing is *hybridity*, how things and ideas are 'repeated, relocated and translated in the name of tradition' (Bhabha, 1995, p. 156; Sanders, 2006, p. 17), and *intertextuality*, 'the permutation of texts by utterances and semiotic signifiers deriving from other texts' (Kristeva, 1980; Sanders, 2006, p. 162). In other words, Shakespeare is as guilty of theft as any other author (Taylor, 1989; Fischlin, 2007).

On the contrary, Brecht used adaptation to criticize the past, condemn Nazi ideologies and promote the ideals of Marxism. Here, adaptation becomes *dialogism* (Carney, 2005, p. 139) – the notion of 'heteroglossia' propounded by anti-Aristotelian Bakhtin as a debate space for social exchange (White, 2009, p. 10) – and thus dialogism becomes *politicization*. Brecht saw the world dialectically and his political theatre entails in this dialectical ontology, as affected by his contact with Marxism during the 1920s (Barnett, 2012, see also Barnett 2015, pp. 18–19). He used adaptation as a political theatre directing methodology, both for the formation of a social exchange space and for the fulfilment of the V-effect, by 'fixing the not-but' of the original texts.

In *The Caucasian Chalk Circle*, Brecht used the Old Testament account of Solomon's threat and German poet Klabund's adaptation of *Circle of Chalk*, a Chinese play by Li Xingdao, to criticize the Nazi organization of society around blood and racial purity and to question the idea of ownership. To do so, Brecht judged the foster mother as the 'true' parent of the child, in addition to the other texts that vindicated the biological mother (Mumford, 2009, p. 101).

Looking back at the history of theatre, one sees that much of the most important and certainly all of the most radical work has been deconstructive – from the indecorous tragedy of Euripides which ridicules and indicts the gods, to Büchner's demonic comedy, to Brecht's non-'Aristotelian', non-cathartic Epic Theatre. The work of these three playwrights was so revolutionary – and remains so – not because it tried to create something wholly new but because

DOI: 10.1057/9781137577047.0007

it worked within history, and within metaphysics, to launch a trenchant critique of the ideology spoken through history and through metaphysics. (Savran, 1986, p. 221)

To launch a trenchant critique, Brecht revisited past texts to converse their ideals, creating a form of *antistrophe adaptation*. Here, adaptation turns into a communication space in-'between two spaces' (White, 2009, p. 6; Moi, 1986, p. 55) – between the old and the new narrative, and the real and mythical. This can also be traced in *He (Who) Said Yes/ He (Who) Said No* (1930), the Brechtian adaptation of the fourteenth-century Japanese Noh drama *Taniko*, where the main character does not respond in accordance with custom, but rather rethinks the question in relation to the new situation presented (Brecht, 1930). Brecht, likewise, rethought the question of ownership in *The Caucasian Chalk Circle* and gave a different answer from the traditional one – an *antistrophe* of the expected – to promote debate on social structures. Thus, by the use of antistrophe adaptation, Brecht created an in-between space for social discussion and exchange.

On the contrary, Brecht used adaptation as a H-effect strategy. Placing the story in a historical, distant time and place, Brecht empowered the audience to make correlations with their own reality. For instance, Brecht's adaptation of Maxim Gorky's 1906 novel, *Mother*, reminded his spectators that 'Communism had already triumphed in Russia and challenged them to fight for a revolutionary solution to Germany's political and economic crisis' (Bradley, 2006, p. 10). Furthermore, in *The Caucasian Chalk Circle*, Brecht mixed old and new artistry and reality with fiction to make a social point. As Mumford (2009, p. 91) notes, in *The Caucasian Chalk Circle* Brecht mixed epic theatre with Aristotelian techniques, and Ancient Greek and Asian mediaeval and folk art with contemporary realism. This collaged form allowed Brecht to transfer the myth in a real, historical, temporal setting – for distancing purposes – of pre-war, soviet Caucasus and the Republic of Georgia after the exodus of Hitler's army (Mumford, 2009, p. 102).

In *Cyberian Chalk Circle*, I use adaptation not to create an antistrophe of the original text's ideologies – it is left to the audience to criticize the story – but rather to get a more in-depth understanding of the play. Thus, in my work, adaptation serves as a 'translation' of meanings in different contexts. Grusha's forced marriage, for instance, is recognized less in Western societies than in Eastern ones. To understand

DOI: 10.1057/9781137577047.0007

and explain why Grusha had to get married to save Michael, I had to place the story in a different cultural setting (of the Middle Eastern world). Hence, in *Cyberian Chalk Circle*, it was the cultural *transposition*, rather than the use of a past temporal setting, that served as a social exchange space and distancing tool. Although I used a contemporary, existing setting for the transposition of the story (to Egypt of 2011), it was the cultural distance ('C-effect') between the character and the audience that served as a V-effect strategy. The C-effect is a fundamental characteristic of this intercultural experiment, where Greek practitioners look at a political situation in the Middle East, through a cyber-New Zealand site, communicating in English with the international audience.

Despite the international character of the audience – especially in CCC2 – the participants identified themselves as 'Westerns': 'Are we educating Westerns here?' (*Cyberian Chalk Circle Part B*, 2011). Although Westerns have some awareness of women's power state in Eastern societies, and the topic seems to be close to the hearts and minds of many, we tend to turn a blind eye in the name of hybridity. In both CCC1 and CCC2, the audience did not know what an *urfi* marriage was: some of the participants searched in real time for the meaning of the word, using Google or Wikipedia. The C-effect enforced discussions regarding the state of women in Western and Eastern societies, a critical comparison between the two worlds (see Figure 3.1), which resulted in the realization that, in the end, they are not as different as they seem or as we want to think.

To recreate the story of Grusha and Simon for the new cultural setting, I used adaptation to devise a specific text-based starting point – the 'stream scene'. Here, I use the term *devise* in its widest sense of a collaborative improvisation, one that promotes ensemble authorship. Owing to the improvisational and interactive character of the Etheatre Project, it was extremely important for the performer to understand her character in depth to be able to answer audience questions and act in different circumstances 'as if' – Stanislavsky's 'magic if' – the character. To research and flesh out the character, Stanislavsky's action analysis method was central during the rehearsal process. Despite the critical attitude towards the system, Brecht acknowledged the importance of Stanislavsky studies for actors' training and as a useful method for acting the *as if* character (Mumford, 2009, p. 152).

DOI: 10.1057/9781137577047.0007

<grusha says> are women safe?
ho is simon
<grusha says> even without a man?
i never heard of urfi marriage before
Depends
Rohipnol
not always
women are not unsafe because they dont have a man
we like to think it is safe
ever
brothers not husbands
But we know otherwise
<grusha says> what is it depending on?
i see a lot of woman walking with digs
I'm not a woman. They sometimes feel unsafe at night I suppose.
Micro-culture you live in
dogs
Quite different.
depending on confidence
<grusha says> not about night and day
on understanding
i usually feel safe, but i have never been attacked
<grusha says> it is always unsafe
on self defence
Look at textual violence occuring against online female journalists in UK and west.
i know women who have been attacked, who never feel safe now
learn wing chun
<grusha says> especially for Michael
it was created by a women
yes it's not all physical violence
<grusha says> i had to do it for him
in the west we have many forms of violence
emotional abuse
<grusha says> i am waiting for you Simon
financial violence
<grusha says> to save us both
wing chun is not violence its counter violence
psychological
According to UN, the Congo is worst place in world to be a woman

FIGURE 3.1    *Text log of* Cyberian Chalk Circle Part B *(2011). Quoted exactly as it stands in the original, the lines beginning with '<grusha says>' are part of the performer's text, while the other lines are typed by anonymous participants.*

Although Brecht himself used Stanislavsky in his work, using the system in Brecht is problematic as the author constantly questions every action of the character. For instance, when Grusha saves Michael, the action suggests both salvation and depredation. However, in order to distance and critically act the character, a performer first needs to research in depth and fully understand the given circumstances.

We first studied the Brechtian Grusha in depth and then used the main elements of the character to build a new Grusha for the Egyptian revolution, in order for Stamatiou to find a balance between Brecht's Russian Grusha and my interpretation of an Egyptian Grusha. Moreover, we examined Grusha's actions and made correlations with the Egyptian reality of 2011. To complete the adapted character and prevent/minimize audience questions, we looked at pragmatic facts, such as Egypt's time zone and weather conditions on the day of the performance and the exact geographical location of the character. Moreover, open rehearsals were planned to help trace audience questions, if any, during the actual performance.

In *Cyberian Chalk Circle*, while text improvisation in the UpStage chat box was the main method during rehearsals to fit the performer into the scene, similarly to how Brecht used improvisation, transformation and adaptation in his writings to 'fit the people he [worked] with' (Lavelli, 1996, p. 116), *real-time* improvisation and interaction with the audience was used during the actual performance. Participants replied critically to the performance materials, opening discussions and holding debates on political topics, 'fixing the not-but' of the adapted text. Cyberformance materializes Brecht's theory of spectating, turning the audience from passive participants to active 'spect-actors', in the sense of Augusto Boal's 'theatre of the oppressed' active audience. According to Kattenbelt, '[t]he clear borderlines that Brecht wanted to draw should create in-between spaces, which the spectator actively needs to fill in' (2008, p. 26).

The audience of *Cyberian Chalk Circle* reviewed the Egyptian revolution by making correlations with their own reality: 'Don't go to Greece maybe it's worse...:-P we must form a rebel alliance' [...] 'They just started to kill each other ...' (Papagiannouli, 2013a, 02:14 min, 02:35 min). As a matter of fact, on 10 May 2011, a 44-year-old Greek man was killed for a camera, while he was accompanying his wife to the hospital for the delivery of their second child. Two days later, an immigrant from Bangladesh was murdered as retaliation for the man's death. Therefore, participants connected the narration of the Egyptian revolution with

DOI: 10.1057/9781137577047.0007

the situation in Greece at that time. *CCC1* realized what Marc Silberman claims to be the task of Brechtian theatre: 'to organize the space or the dialogical situation in a larger framework which allows a new subjectivity, which allows us to begin to define a new individual and collective subject' (1987, p. 460).

Moreover, different opinions were exposed during the performances of *Cyberian Chalk Circle*, shaping debates on specific themes. In *CCC1*, Act III: The Secret Marriage, when the performer (Grusha) asked whether women in the audience's country have to get married to be able to live with a man, one of the participants replied that in their country women can live without men, and have children, but society does not always accept it, while another one stated that 'women can do what they want. They fuck each other all around' (Papagiannouli, 2013b, 01:50–02:55 min).

Apart from text interactions with the performer, participants commented on each other's posts during the performance, playing the role of Brechtian clowns:

> When I get a theater into my clutches, I will hire two clowns. They enter the stage between acts acting as spectators. They exchange views about the play and the audience and conclude bets about the end of the play.... In a tragedy, the scenery will be changed with open curtains. Clowns walk across the stage and order: 'Now he (the hero) will fall, yes. Lower the lights.' (Brecht, quoted in Schoeps, 1995, p. 49)

In *CCC1* when one of the audience members lied to Grusha that Simon got married, someone else responded 'Shame on you!' (Papagiannouli, 2013b, 12:35 min), while in *CCC2* (Part B) when someone said that Simon will return home soon, an audience member replied 'Don't give her hope/ he might be...not well' (*Cyberian Chalk Circle Part B*, 2011). Brecht wanted the audience to enter the theatre space and behave as if in a circus, boxing ring or racecourse rather than as if they had entered a temple. The anonymity of online spectating not only protects the real identities of the participants but also promotes such behaviour in cyberformance (trolling), as the audience can demonstrate their real character without hiding behind social masks and decorous behaviour: 'Man is least himself when he talks in his own person. Give him a mask, and he will tell you the truth' (Wilde, 2007, p. 83).

The *Cyberian Chalk Circle* text was written in real time, during the performance, with participants' help, who either knew or did not know the original play; prior knowledge was not important for participating in the show: although cyberformance is an experimental form of theatre, spectators do not need to be theatre or computer experts to participate, as it uses simple online tools that people use in everyday life. John Ellis (1982) rightly underlines that adaptation exists in the memory of the original text, either in the form of a generally circulated memory or derived from the actual reading of the text (see also Sanders, 2006, p. 25). This should be considered in adaptations, and especially in interactive adaptations where the flow of a performance is highly dependent on spectators' participation. In *CCC1*, for instance, one of the participants, who evidently knew the original play, asked questions about Michael and Grusha's marriage before Grusha mentioned anything about it. This resulted in a quicker flow of the performance to the next scenes, making some participants believe that I (the director) was behind the anonymity of those questions and, hence, that the performance was being controlled.

The adapted scene was thus *re*-adapted by the participants. The audience wrote the dialogues, directed the actor and influenced the turn of the performance, by commenting on each scenario. From this, one can conclude that cyberformance opens up new open-ended possibilities for adaptation, using the Internet as a space for real-time adaptation and playwriting. Similarly to the ensemble work of Brecht, who wrote and re-wrote his text during rehearsals or after the performance, text-based cyberformance offers a new form of real-time writing through collaboration, allowing for audience engagement in the process of writing and adapting the text.

The *spaceless* characteristic of the cyberstage produced the V-effect, allowing participants to critically engage with the performance and make real-time connections between the storytelling and their own reality. Cyberformance allows the creation of such dialectical methodologies in theatre directing. In *Cyberian Chalk Circle*, the participants tested and interrogated the character/performer through the text box; they could challenge the performer by asking the character any questions they wanted. In the Etheatre Project, the use of the Internet enforced active participation of the audience in the performance, thereby breaking the fourth wall. While the audience themselves 'fixed the not-but', 'whatever [the actor] doesn't do must be contained and conserved in what he does. In this way every sentence and every gesture signifies a decision; the character remains under observation and is tested' (Brecht, 1964c [1933], p. 137). Key examples include: 'violence is not the solution [ ... ], but silence is not either' (*Cyberian Chalk Circle Part A*, 2011); 'who wouldn't protect a child? [ ... ] A great many paedophiles or child abusers, that's who wouldn't'; 'Posing ethical questions that no one can answer out of context. [...] Good to pose the questions, even if there is no answer. [...] Its [*sic*] not that there are no answers, people have answers, but what relevance has it to real events?' (*Cyberian Chalk Circle Part B*, 2011).

### 3.1.1   Staging *Cyberian Chalk Circle*

The 'beta' version – the testing version of a computer programme – of the Etheatre Project was a 60-minute, one-off show that looked at the political character of the Internet. The participants, who were mainly Greek, were invited – via Facebook, Twitter and email – to sit comfortably in their desk, chair or sofa, on their bed or even in their local café, and follow the show while continuing to update their Twitter feed, chat on Skype, spy on their friends on Facebook or just search for something on Google. Acknowledging the difficulty of concentrating in an online platform – a 'hard to focus place' (Haug, 2012) – without efficient multitasking, the test show aimed to prevent audience reactions and invert the expectations of a classic theatre experience, highlighting that the performance would take place online and that there was no need to travel to a theatre space. Although the invitation clearly stated the performance would be *online*, some audience members replied that they would not be able to attend the performance as they were based in Greece; even when explained in detail, it was difficult especially for theatre practitioners to understand how this 'online theatre' would work. This raised concerns regarding audience understanding of the platform and the level of engagement during the performance.

Contrary to my concerns, however, the audience started chatting with each other even before the performance began – initially using the text box for foyer-like discussions, counting down time till the beginning of the show – and continued their conversations for at least 40 minutes after the performance ended. According to Brecht, theatre representations, by taking second place to what is presented, leave the audience 'productively disposed' even after the end of the event (1964d [1949], p. 205). This completes Meike Wagner and Wolf-Dieter Ernst's 'no starting point, no ending [point]' analysis of a theatre performance (2010, p. 178), drawing on Bruno Latour's actor-network theory:

> According to Latour, a network is not considered to be a built or communicated 'thing'; rather one has to think of a network as a conceptual perspective. This perspective implies, that any analysis of a network cannot be conducted

from the outside, because the 'object' of observation, i.e. the actor-network, changes in the process of its analysis. It does so, because, among other influences, it reacts to the movement the beholder or observer causes in the process of his or her analysis, his or her moving around within the actor-network. That is to say, an actor network only exists when it is constructed through the process of reading. (Wagner and Ernst, 2010, p. 178)

*CCC1*, in this respect, began not on 14 May 2011 but a week earlier, when the first participant entered the cyberstage and used the chat box to communicate. Once I announced the platform of the performance, potential participants followed the link and some, out of curiosity, used the chat box. Once they had written something they could not erase it, as it became part of the performance text for the next participant. Similarly, *CCC1* finished when the last audience member left the cyberstage and I cleared the stage and the chat box, turning UpStage again into a blank canvas, an empty stage to mark the end of the performance. Otherwise, any visitor to the webpage would be able to read the contents of the performance discussion and reply in the chat box.

*CCC1* was a three-act show. Act I, named 'Grusha and Simon', reflected the peaceful past of the character: Grusha's life before the revolution. The audience got a more complete idea of the character by learning key information about Grusha's social life, such as that she had got engaged to Simon and that she worked for the governor. In Act II, 'The Revolution', Grusha introduced a new character, Michael. In the beginning she narrated chaotic images of the revolution and described how she had lost Simon and how she had found Michael. Then, she explained why it was not safe for her to keep the boy, why Michael was unsafe and what she had to do for them to stay safe. In Act III, 'The Secret Marriage', Grusha asked the audience to help her find Simon and explain to him why she had married someone else. The performance finished with Simon's appearance in the chat box and the failure of Grusha's Internet connection. Simon wrote Grusha's full name for recognition to take place – Aristotle's notion of *anagnorisis* that indicates a change from ignorance to knowledge for good to bad fortune (MacFarlane, 2000). To perform the connection failure, I reset the stage button, taking the stage back to its original state. The reset button in UpStage works as a virus, reloading all browsers that are linked to the stage. When the participants re-entered the platform, after their browser's automatic refresh, Grusha was missing. However, many of the participants did not experience the ending as described, as they were still on Facebook or another platform,

DOI: 10.1057/9781137577047.0007

and they missed the *anagnorisis* and 'reload scene'. As a result, each participant experienced the finale of the performance differently.

Following the *CCC1* performance, *CCC2*, neatly coinciding with Armistice Day (11 November), was the reproduction of *CCC1* for the 11:11:11 UpStage Festival. Affected by the Remembrance Day special celebrations in the United Kingdom and New Zealand, where the festival is based, instead of by the political character of the Internet, the performance questioned what we have learnt since the horrors of World War I, combining similar images of horror from World War I and the Egyptian revolution. Although the events are not connected, the juxtaposition reminded the participants that 'war is a terrible thing, no matter where in the world it is happening' (audience comment from the Etheatre Project blog). The two-part performance of *CCC2* began with Part A on 11 November 2011, from 11:00 to 11:30 a.m. New Zealand time, and finished with Part B, from 10:30 to 11:00 a.m. UK time, on the same day. This allowed *CCC2* to open with a two-minute silence marking Remembrance Day in New Zealand and to end with a two-minute silence marking the day in the United Kingdom.

Unlike the three-act breakdown of the first performance, *CCC2* was a four-act show. Part A consisted of Act I: 'Grusha and Simon' and Act II: 'The Revolution'; Part B consisted of Act III: 'Grusha and Michael' and Act IV: 'The Secret Marriage'. Part B focused more on Grusha's sacrifices for Michael, enhancing the boy's presence in a separate act (Act III), which was merely decorative in *CCC1*. This allowed a circular structuring of the performance, where the same motive of the revolution was repeated to mark, at first, loss and, then, salvation. In Part A Grusha loses Simon, while in Part B she finds Michael; both events are because of the revolution. I used the same backdrops in both parts, changing only the sounds surrounding the images: in Part A the chaotic sound of white noise was played, whereas in Part B the playful sound of water drops was used.

In particular, in Part A, Grusha narrated how she had met Simon, got engaged and then how she had lost him because of the revolution; she asked the audience to find Simon and tell him to come and meet her on the UpStage platform in about ten hours (in time for Part B). To explain the durational gap between the two parts, due to the time zone difference between the countries, Part A finished with Grusha leaving the platform concerned about her husband's arrival, thus revealing her marriage to the audience without giving further explanations. The objective of this

DOI: 10.1057/9781137577047.0007

was also to give a clear sense that *CCC2* was a 'to be continued' performance and to excite the audience's curiosity to make them return for the
second part.

Inspired by the 'We Are All Khaled Said' case, where online support
was gathered via a Facebook page of the same name commemorating a
28-year-old Egyptian (Khaled Said) who was tortured to death by two
police officers in Egypt, in Part B the audience collectively represented
Simon. As Grusha was not sure whether Simon was there – most of
the audience told her that they had found him but they were not sure
whether he was coming – she responded to the participants as if *they*
were Simon. Grusha, hoping that Simon was one of the anonymous
responders, explained how she had met Michael and what she had to do
to keep him safe, closing with the revelation of the *urfi* marriage. Now
the audience could see Grusha's face (Figure 3.2).

When a (cyber)performance is split over days or hours, the consistency of the audience cannot be controlled, as not all the participants
are able to return or new audience members who have not followed the
previous episode appear. In the case of *CCC2*, this influenced negatively
the consistency of the show. Despite the positive contribution of familiar
participants who played the role of the narrator and explained to new

FIGURE 3.2    *Screenshot of a webcam avatar taken during UpStage 11:11:11 at
11:33:17 a.m. (CCC2, Part B).*

DOI: 10.1057/9781137577047.0007

audience members what preceded in Part A (although Part B's introduction operated mainly as a précis of Part A), some new participants still could not follow the plot. Furthermore, audience members who participated only in the first part did not get to see how Grusha really looks as the webcast avatar did not work owing to technical problems.

The blank stage in Part A influenced the level of audience engagement, as the audience did not participate as actively as in Part B. Another factor that affected the participation of spectators in CCC2 was the festive character of the show: the audience was invited to watch the next performance, which started straight after the end of each part. Although flexibility is essential in participative forms of theatre like cyberformance, consistency remains key for the story to unfold. In *Cyberian Chalk Circle*, 'safe scenes' or transaction scenes had been pre-prepared allowing movement from one topic to another using tableau aesthetics. For instance, when the flow of participation fell in the introduction of Grusha and Simon's meeting and love story, the performer continued to the next scene and began the storytelling of the revolution.

CCC3, performed on Waterwheel Tap, was an open rehearsal aiming to pre-test the new platform for the second venture of the Etheatre Project. Despite its informal character and the small number of audience – five connected computers – CCC3 had great significance for the Etheatre Project. First, it completed a circle of experimentation regarding the online staging of *Cyberian Chalk Circle*. Second, the 20-minute open rehearsal developed further the idea of using the participants as Simon's representatives. In CCC3, the 'stream scene' was staged on Waterwheel Tap with the audience playing the character of Simon. Grusha connected with the audience via the web stream, but she also used the chat box when she wanted to say something secretly, so no one else could hear her. Finally, the audience comprised cyberformance experts – I invited Waterwheel Tap performers to watch the open rehearsal and contribute – whose after-performance comments were crucial for the development of the next Etheatre Project.

## 3.2    Cyber-ethnotheatre: *Merry Crisis and a Happy New Fear*

Apart from using cyber-ethnography as a data collection tool for the exploration of human communication, social interaction and conflict, I also used it as a method to analyse the collected data in a performative way. In the second experiment of the Etheatre Project, *Merry Crisis and a Happy New Fear* (2012), pre-collected answers to an online questionnaire[2] were used as a performance text, which focused on the memory of the participants in relation to the murder of Alexandros Grigoropoulos. Following the first project, *Merry Crisis and a Happy New Fear* was a verbatim Christmas story about the collapse of Greek democracy. On 6 December 2008, policeman Epaminondas Korkoneas killed Alexandros Grigoropoulos, a 15-year-old student, in the Exarcheia district of central Athens. The unjust murder of the young schoolboy by police resulted in large protests and demonstrations, which escalated to widespread rioting, with hundreds of rioters damaging property and engaging riot police with Molotov cocktails, stones and other objects. A new wish jumped up from the embers of those nights, 'Merry Crisis and a Happy New Fear', opening a Pandora's box of the Greek economy and the unstable political situation of the country.

The online questionnaire aimed to collect individual memories to create a performance about the collective memory of the real event, what Gilles Deleuze describes as a 'world memory' or the globalized memory of an event as shaped by the media (quoted in Bennett and Kennedy, 2003, pp. 5–6). Indeed, most of the participants knew about the murder because 'it was on the news' or they had 'read it in the newspaper' or 'on the Internet'. However, few respondents had a more personal connection with the event, giving a different interpretation to the memory:

> TOM: Some friends called me from Athens, and told me what happened. After the call and a conversation with friends we learned more details and we heard about a meeting in university. In the meeting, we decided to protest in the streets for the murder of Alex by the policeman, against the police and the government. [ ... ]
> ANN: My daily routine changed because of the protesters but generally I was confused.[3]

The questionnaire responses 'fixed the not-but' of the performance text by offering different viewpoints for the same event. Furthermore, they also helped to cast the audience, by giving an understanding of what the participants might know about the event before the actual performance. I edited the collected responses to craft the performance script, which the performers (Ann Cross and Tom Mangan) read one after the other in real time, incorporating answers the online audience gave during the performance.

DOI: 10.1057/9781137577047.0007

Here, cyber-ethnography took the form of cyber-ethnotheatre. Ethnotheatre is a performance-based ethnographic method constituted by a dramatic event, such as a live performance, that uses data collected by a researcher as performance material (Leavy, 2009, p. 144). As Duška Radosavljević notes, 'ethnotheatre' is the US term for verbatim theatre (2013, p. 121). Verbatim is a popular documentary theatre form in the United Kingdom that uses word-by-word interview recordings as a performance text. Although the two terms define the same kind of performance, an intermedial genre between research and theatre, the term ethnotheatre is used mainly for research purposes, whereas verbatim theatre is used for performance practices.

According to David Hare, '[verbatim theatre] does what journalism fails to do' (quoted in Hammond and Steward, 2008, p. 62): to uncover hidden interpretations of reality and give space to unheard voices to be heard. Interestingly, the recent wave of 'new journalism', also called 'online journalism', also aims to cover the gap of old journalism by using the Internet as a platform for objective information and interactive communication with the audience (Darras et al., 2013). The Internet offers spaces for such political movements (as proved in the Turkish Spring example in Chapter 1), allowing a more objective approach towards truth through crowd-funding and audience engagement. However, both verbatim theatre and new journalism, especially blogs, have been ethically accused of being selective: 'Verbatim theatre is as selective in its use of material as TV's Big Brother. It's just that, sitting in a theatre, we are often all too willing to suspend our disbelief' (Gardner, 2009). In verbatim cyberformance, apart from pre-recorded material, participants share their own beliefs in real time.

*Merry Crisis and a Happy New Fear* combined verbatim theatre and an online platform for real-time audience interaction with the event. Here, the audience completed the performance text by responding to the questionnaire in the text box during the performance, while performers incorporated phrases from the text box into the pre-existing script, editing the performance text in real time. By mixing pre-recorded and real-time videos, and pre-recorded answers with real-time audience responses, *Merry Crisis and a Happy New Fear* challenged the notion of *liveness* and broke the fourth wall by applying Brecht's montage strategy. Apart from montage aesthetics, the Etheatre Project also used tableau strategies to create the V-effect. The performance was broken into four scenes in relation to questions asked to the audience. Scene 1 introduced

DOI: 10.1057/9781137577047.0007

the story background and the participants; Scene 2 was based on the question 'Where were you on 6 December 2008 at 9:00 p.m.?'; Scene 3 sought answers to 'How did you find out about the boy's murder?' and 'What did you do after 6 December 2008?'; and Scene 4 aimed to make the audience focus on the title slogan, asking the audience to 'Make a wish for the New Year [2013]' (see *Merry Crisis and a Happy New Fear*, 2012).

Technology is central here not only for the collection of audience memories and real-time interaction but also for presenting the absence of the 'real people who were interviewed' (Hutchison, 2009, p. 210). The performers' webcams fade out and in simultaneously, to represent both the absence of storytellers and the faded character of memories. Furthermore, I used the real, unprofessional video of the murder, as uploaded on YouTube by a witness the next day, to represent the absence of the murdered protagonist (GiaNtakos, 2008). Since that night, the video has been reproduced in the news, in blogs, in documentary films and even in court, thus turning into a performative. In *Merry Crisis and a Happy New Fear*, the representation of the video evidenced the real character of the story.

The commemorating character of the performance theme – the performance aimed to remind the audience of a specific event and generate discussions using collected memories of individuals – led me to cast two performers who were interested in the topic of protest as theatre, with previous experience in political, documentary and verbatim theatre from the same generation as Grigoropoulos (born in the 1990s) and who had recently experienced the student protests of 2010 in the United Kingdom. To help the performers understand and engage with the Greek protests of 2008, we looked at the student demonstrations of 2010 and the riots of 2011 in the United Kingdom that followed the death of Mark Duggan after a police officer shot him. The correlation between the different events helped us to analyse the answers of the questionnaire during our first meetings where we closely looked at the script of the performance.

Technical rehearsals followed our political discussions to introduce performers to the platform and its tools. Although the technical rehearsals were face-to-face, remote Waterwheel experts attended the tutorials to assist with technical problems. For instance, we had to deal with a 'ghost camera' bug, which allowed us to hear the performers but not to see their streaming avatars, and a 'double streaming' bug, which blocked the performers from seeing their own streaming, but compelling them to see two streaming avatars of a fellow performer. For this reason, I

DOI: 10.1057/9781137577047.0007

created a mirror Tap platform to use on the day of the performance in case of similar technical problems.

Once the performers familiarized themselves with the technical features of the platform, we rehearsed the script in a theatrical manner working on the reading flow of the text. At first, we read through the script together; then the performers read their respective lines one after the other. Thereafter, each performer read the whole script once, including the lines of fellow performers. Finally, they read their own lines aloud and fellow performers' lines silently, simultaneously. These exercises helped the performers to understand the rhythm of the text and get comfortable with it. This was important because the performers had to mix live audience responses in the chat box with the given script in real time during the performance.

We also worked with the webcam, exploring different movements the performers could use to ensure a more physical presence on the cyberstage, and experimented with the streaming effects of the platform. While the actors were performing their movements, I worked on improving and finalizing the technical features and webcam effects. We used physical movements and effects mainly for transitional moments. Ann Cross and Tom Mangan (the performers I collaborated with), for instance, performed a physical act of a gunshot, shooting each other, to move from the introductory part to the second part, while I moved the focus of the webcams from one to the other and used fade-in and fade-out effects to mark their cue changes. We repetitively worked on the physical movements to help the performers feel confident with them and with the 'backwards' image of the streaming – where the performers' right side was reflected to the left of the stage by the webcam.

However, *Merry Crisis and a Happy New Fear* cannot be considered a successful experiment in terms of audience political and dialectical participation and engagement, thus proving that a participatory performance is not necessarily a political performance. Although audience members answered questions via the chat box, further debate on the topic was not achieved. This is mainly because of the disrupted communication between performers and participants, who were based in different cyberstage places – the performers in the streaming avatars and the audience in the chat box – and because the performance script did not allow in-depth interaction with the audience. In political cyberformances, real-time improvisational scenes are central to facilitating discussion between performers and audience members, something that was not achieved

DOI: 10.1057/9781137577047.0007

here because of the tightness of the script. This also affected the duration of the performance, which could not outrun 20 minutes.

## 3.3    Cyber-collaboration: *Etheatre Project and Collaborators*

The Etheatre Project is the outcome of a collaborative process that embraced the audience as part of the ensemble. The Internet turned into a collective space for real-time collaboration, engagement and exchange. In a cyberformance, online platforms allow a new form of remote cyber-collaboration to take place, between the audience and the performance and between the performers themselves. As a result, audience participation retains a key role in the making and staging of a cyberformance, where participants can interact with the performance and become part of the collective ensemble of the company. In a cyberformance, the audience can manifest themselves and choose whether or not they want to collaborate, stay silent or take active part in the happenings. Here, Brecht's spect-actor meets Boal's spect-actor, allowing a critical participation and engagement with the performance. Cyberformance creates in-between spaces for the audience to actively fill in, what Kattenbelt (2008) describes as the Brechtian borderlines. The notion of cyber-collaboration and audience participation in cyberformance entails co-presence in the sense of 'temporal and spatial proximity between performer and audience' (Fewster, 2010a, p. 46; Lehmann, 2006, pp. 141–42). The originality of the Etheatre Project collaborations lies in their geographical distance and the use of the Internet as a political space for collaboration and co-creation.

The main methodological attitude of the Etheatre Project was its creative practice. According to Jamieson, using the creative process as a research methodology 'opens up the possibility for unexpected opportunities along the way – something that is crucial when experimenting with new technologies and in an emerging art form' (2008, p. 11). Jamieson's 'haphazard creative process' allowed the Etheatre Project to collaborate with cyberformance experts for the realization of its performances, such as the remote collaboration with the UpStage and Waterwheel Tap platform coordinators. I also collaborated with professional actors. More specifically, for all three *Cyberian Chalk Circle* performances, I worked with Stamatiou, while Tsinikoris kindly sponsored photographs for Simon's Facebook account; for the *Merry Crisis and a Happy New*

DOI: 10.1057/9781137577047.0007

*Fear* project, I collaborated with Cross and Mangan. The most recent *Etheatre Project and Collaborators* is the outcome of cyber-collaborating with seven international artists and cyberformers (Sarahleigh Castelyn, Charis Gavriilidis, Evi Stamatiou, Ilinca Tamara Todorut, Suzon Fuks, Marischka Klinkhamer and Anca Donzi) based in the United States, Australia, United Kingdom, Germany and the Netherlands.

The Etheatre Project's collaborations, in turn, affected the creative practice, which adapted itself in relation to platform requirements. In *Merry Crisis and a Happy New Fear*, I injected the 'water' concept of the platform, as required by Waterwheel Tap's statute, connecting it to the 'human rivers' that overflowed the streets in Greece during the 2008 protests for the unjust murder of Grigoropoulos. Moreover, the date of the 11:11:11 UpStage Festival played a crucial role for the context of the performance that combined the revolution in Egypt with Remembrance Day celebrations. The platform's tools also affected the outcome of the performances, which influenced the text-based character of the Etheatre Project.

In *Cyberian Chalk Circle*, the limitations of the UpStage platform were also used as a tool to create a 'slow Internet connection' effect for the participants and to represent the difficulty in communication during the revolution in Egypt. Hence, instead of live streaming, snapshots from the performer's webcam were uploaded to UpStage every second, creating the sense of a bad connection, enhanced by the robotic computer-generated voice that read aloud the performer's text in the chat box. The computer voice also contributed to the production of the V-effect, as its flat way of speaking was 'free from parsonical sing-song and from all those cadences which lull the spectator so that the sense gets lost' (Brecht, 1964d [1949], p. 193).

Cyberformance platforms promote real-time collaboration by using digital tools. Waterwheel Tap allows mixing of real-time video streaming, offering options such as move, rotate, resize, fade in or out, bring forward or take backwards, flip horizontal or vertical and hide the web-streaming avatar or the uploaded video avatar. Moreover, both Waterwheel Tap and UpStage provide a palette for real-time drawing and a text box for real-time writing. Performers can use the given tools for co-creation, turning the Internet into a collaboration space. *Merry Crisis and a Happy New Fear*, for instance, ended with a real-time collective drawing made by the performers and me.

Furthermore, the use of specialized, non-public digital platforms required collaboration with experts in the field. Training is important for artists to learn how to use the various platforms. Although Waterwheel Tap and UpStage have published instructions for use, the complexity of the platforms led to following tutorials with experts. Collaborating with experts is also important as technology failure is a key part of cyber-formance. In both *Cyberian Chalk Circle* and *Merry Crisis and a Happy New Fear*, technical problems arose that could not have been overcome without the support of the platforms' experts.

For instance, in Part B of *CCC2*, a mirror stage of the cyberstage provided by the festival organizers was used, in order to use the webcasting tool that was not working in Part A. However, the audience still could not see the webcam avatar in full screen as in *CCC1*. This was because in *CCC2* the position of the webcam was found to be dependent on the web browser of each spectator. Hence, to ensure that all participants could see Grusha clearly, a smaller frame was used (see Figure 3.2). Having an alternative plan, a 'plan B', is crucial when working with technology. Thus, in *CCC2* we were much better prepared for a technical failure. Grusha made clear to the audience that the connection may fail at any minute and asked participants to wait for her (in such an event) until she reconnected; a 'connection failure' flash backdrop was also prepared, making the technical failure a part of the performance.

On the contrary, the performers also influenced the creative practice of the Etheatre Project. The interactive and improvisational character of both *Cyberian Chalk Circle* and *Merry Crisis and a Happy New Fear* allowed space for the performers' own interpretations, turning actors to spect-actors in the Brechtian meaning of the distancing performer (Mumford, 2009, p. 175). Brecht's theatre requires performers to critically review and demonstrate a character's behaviour from a social point of view. To do so, Brechtian spect-actors have to be distant from the character they act out, simultaneously in-between critical spectating and acting. To empower the dialectical aesthetics of Brecht and 'fix the not-but' – Brecht's strategy to identify contradictions between the actor and the character (Mumford, 2009, pp. 66–67) – performance text lines were studied to try to discover the meanings of the text from the very beginning of performance rehearsals. Face-to-face discussions were held about the different situations the characters faced, questioning specific actions.

In cyberformance, dialectical aesthetics are accomplished by the cyber-collaboration of the audience and performers in real time. Since work on the UpStage platform began, rehearsals of *Cyberian Chalk Circle* were open to the public to help prepare the performer for any reaction. People were invited to join the rehearsals, taking an active role by commenting and asking questions, and play the role of the inspiring audience – the Brechtian clown who challenges the performance by not following theatrical contracts. Brecht used to keep his rehearsals open, for actors to get used to spectators, and start working with an audience as early in the process as possible (Weber and Munk, 1967–68). In interactive performances, open rehearsals are crucial for performer familiarization and preparation for audience reactions, especially in cyberformances where spectators' interaction remains anonymous.

Apart from the remote collaboration with the audience during rehearsals, the performers also collaborated remotely for the purposes of this study. Although most of the rehearsals were face to face, as everyone was based in London and could share the same geographical space, collaborations and performances were also organized remotely from different spaces. For the second show of *Merry Crisis and a Happy New Fear*, each of the performers and audience was connected to Waterwheel Tap from his/her own house. Despite the communication gap and the ensuing difficulties in communicating with each other – for internal communication, the Waterwheel Tap performers' text box, Skype and mobile phones (in case of Internet connection failure) were used – remote staging could be accomplished successfully in cyberspace.

For the last Etheatre Project, *Etheatre Project and Collaborators*, I collaborated remotely with international artists and cyberformance experts to stage a cyberformance on UpStage for the platform's 10th birthday celebrations on 9 January 2014. Using the topic of internal European migration as a starting point – the topic opened up the notion of migration in general as the collaborators were based across the world – and the new features of UpStage v3 (streaming, avatar drawing and applause button), this third project was a devised, collaborative, site-specific performance open to audience participation and interaction. During the creative process, apart from the UpStage stage, a Facebook group was used as a basic communication platform to meet and brainstorm about the topic. The Facebook group became the primary platform for the team to meet, share stories, exchange ideas and explore and build the performance context. Piratepad, for text editing and text sharing, and Skype, for one-to-one meetings between the director and the creative team (mainly the scenographer and the dramaturg) were also used. To arrange rehearsals and meetings on UpStage, we used the Doodle scheduling tool.

DOI: 10.1057/9781137577047.0007

In August 2013, Helen Varley Jamieson and Vicki Smith invited me to stage a political cyberformance on UpStage v3 for the platform's birthday event (Jamieson, 2013b). Two months later, I approached fellow UpStagers, former collaborators and colleagues with an open call to create 'a completely remote "situation" process' (Jamieson, 2013d). Although I initially wanted to keep the call as open as possible, without limiting it to a specific theme – ideally, the collaborators would have taken active part in deciding the topic, similarly to NTW's democratic process – Jamieson rightly suggested that people would be more likely to get involved when a central idea of interest to them exists (Jamieson, 2013c). Indeed, the topic of European internal migration allowed collaborators to bring in their own ideas and shape the performance topic for the needs of the group, stretching the theme to 'migration' as a general concept.

In cyber-collaboration, the existence of an online group page is key for collaborators to meet and exchange ideas. Soon after Etheatre Project collaborators agreed to take part in this process or showed some interest in engaging with the project, I created the 'Etheatre Project III' Facebook closed group to welcome the artists and introduce them to each other. Since the process was completely remote, the personal Facebook pages of the artists helped group members get an idea of each other's virtual self. At first, we used the Facebook group to share articles about European internal migration. Although the collaborators seemed to read and 'like' the articles, they did not engage in further discussion on the topic. So, to hold the group's interest and assist discussion and reflection on the theme, I posted a note introducing myself within the context of migration:

Dear Collaborators,

Let's introduce ourselves to each other... most of us (if not all) are 'travellers'. We were born in different countries (or towns) from where we live now and we went to school in different places from where we study or work. Let's draw our life journey in relation to geographical places... as what would be more interesting to discuss about 'migration' than our own personal journey stories? [ ... ]

Hope this inspires you to share your own stories and thoughts... Looking forward to your contributions. (Papagiannouli, 2013c)

This immediately motivated the whole group to share personal stories, implicitly offering ideas for the piece. For instance, most of the personal migration stories used the term 'home' in different ways, leading to

DOI: 10.1057/9781137577047.0007

the question: 'What makes *home, home?*' – a question that became the curtain cue for the *Etheatre Project and Collaborators* performance. In the first Skype meeting with dramaturg Ilinca Tamara Todorut, we decided to edit the text shared by the collaborators and create a first script for the performance, which we then re-edited after rehearsals to fit the needs of the performers and the performance piece. I also circulated the text via Piratepad for the whole group to access the script, allowing performers to edit their own lines. Although we did not use Piratepad intensively, it functioned as an archival space that documented changes in the script.

Following the personalized character of the first post, I asked project participants to share pictures of objects that can be carried in a suitcase when one moves/relocates (for the avatars) and pictures of things that cannot be carried (for the backdrops) and to explain individual choices. Although these posts aimed to collect inspiration for set (avatars and backdrops) design, they also influenced the script. This became central to the outcome of the piece, where the objects – such as the ring, the box and the pot – acquired a voice and shared their own stories.

The performers used makeshift rings and pots as avatars for initial improvisations until the dress rehearsal. Owing to time zone differences, it was very difficult to arrange common rehearsals for the dramaturg and the scenographer, who were based in the United States and Australia, respectively. As a result, the dramaturg attended the first set of rehearsals until the completion of a script sequence and the scenographer attended the final ones, where the audiovisual needs of the piece were much clearer after the performance structure/script was blocked. An open general rehearsal (*prova generale*) followed on 8 January 2014, where collaborators, UpStagers and audience members were invited to attend and comment on the performance.

Time zone difference is an important issue in any cyberformance and/ or remote collaboration. Although most of the participants were based in Europe (Germany, the Netherlands, Greece and the United Kingdom), it was still difficult to arrange and coordinate rehearsals, and so we used Doodle, which measures time differences and allows users to read time-tables based on their geographical location. This also helped to manage the needs of the whole group, as each member could vote for the most convenient rehearsal time and the platform highlighted the best option(s).

The first two meetings on UpStage (on 30 November and 11 December 2013) introduced the collaborators to UpStage v3 and guided them through the different tools of the platform, such as drawing, streaming,

DOI: 10.1057/9781137577047.0007

avatar and backdrop controls. All collaborators were invited to attend these tutorials, which helped them gain a hands-on understanding of the features of UpStage – they also had access to the UpStage v3 draft manual (see UpStage 2013) prior to the rehearsals. The performers were subsequently provided with login accounts and were encouraged to experiment and play with the tools freely on the Etheatre Project UpStage cyberstage. This would help to reduce differences between cyberformance experts and less-experienced collaborators. On the rehearsals that followed, we worked on the performance script.

The less text a cyberformance script has the better it is for audience interaction and flow of performance, as proved by the unsuccessful experiment of the highly verbal *Merry Crisis and a Happy New Fear* production. Once the dramaturg finalized the first draft of the script, we started working on the text with the performers. They first typed through – instead of reading through – the script, in the chat box, and then improvised on text themes, scene by scene. The performers' improvisation in the chat box not only highlighted the most powerful bits of the script but also revealed new topics for discussion. By the end of this process, we replaced most of the script with topics for real-time improvisation during the performance to allow space for audience interaction and performer–audience discussion. The text of the final script aimed to facilitate discussion and functioned as cues that linked the different improvisational scenes – the backbone of the performance.

To showcase what can be done with UpStage and cyberformance in general, I had to incorporate all the different UpStage tools in the production. Although I believe that in political cyberformance directing less is more and the simpler the better, the polyphony of the *Etheatre Project and Collaborators* piece helped me to illuminate the different sides of (e)migration and draw out the process behind the piece in a 30-minute performance. The opening backdrop showing the statistics about migration exposed the dark side of the topic as gathered from different media and articles we looked at as a group at the beginning of the process. However, the closing backdrop uncovered the personal character of the performance, stating that 'there are 232 million people living outside their country of birth [as noted by United Nations Secretary-General Ban Ki-moon (2013) on International Migrants Day], [and] 8 of them are actively participating in this project'. The streaming avatars – which did not work during the performance – aimed to uncover step by step the people behind the stories, beginning with only the images of the performers and

DOI: 10.1057/9781137577047.0007

then the real sounds of their voices, as the audience would be able to hear only the computer-generated voice of the avatars at this point. This was important for the piece as it would not only assist audience interaction but also highlight the authenticity of the characters and their stories. To balance the negative aspects of the discussion on migration we used drawings and sounds of whales and birds to demonstrate the positive effects of a natural migration (Figure 3.3). The performance concluded with the avatars exhibiting the nostalgic character of migration, looking at memories, people and places left behind when moving – a central idea in our investigation of the topic as a group.

In cyber-collaboration, the main job of the cyberformance director is to manage the group and be ready to make decisions when needed (most importantly, in real time). The role of the director as a facilitator is also evidenced here, as the director should be ready to assist members of the group and find constructive solutions to problems that may arise during the rehearsal process. Although a cyber-collaborative piece is the outcome of group/teamwork, the role of the director is critical in negotiating between different features of a production, such as technical and artistic, and in maintaining a linear character throughout the devised creative piece.

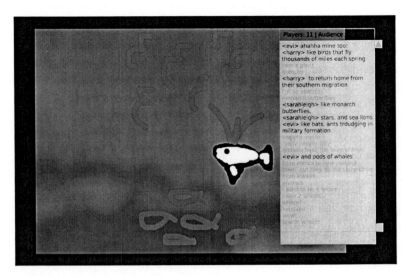

FIGURE 3.3    *Screenshot showing the whales and birds drawn to demonstrate positive natural migration* (Etheatre Project and Collaborators, *09:30 CET, 09:39 min*).

DOI: 10.1057/9781137577047.0007

## 3.4    Directing absence: strategies of co-presence embodiment on cyberstage

In cyberformance, the ethnography of online spaces needs to be studied in accordance with surrounding offline spaces and events. According to Lisa Law, the Internet as an innovative mode of transnational communication helps to 'shape political spaces that exist in symbiotic relation to the "real"' (2011, p. 240). The direct relationship between online and offline activity can be traced in the first two Etheatre Project performances, where the audience reflected on this coexistence and used the online space as a representation of the 'real' by making correlations with their own reality.

Brecht's intention was to create an effective representation of contemporary reality on stage, while making obvious to the audience that what they observe is *theatre* and not a *real* representation of life. The Etheatre Project demonstrates that this 'to be and not to be' aspect of the Brechtian V-effect exists in the theatrical use of the cyberspace as a cyberstage. The *Cyberian Chalk Circle* performance, reflecting on this coexistence, reinforced the dialectical relationship between the virtual and the real, by combining digital tools with theatrical conventions for the embodiment of the absent presence of cyberspace.

The final section of this study examines the nature of presence in cyberformance – an in-between absence and presence situation – and outlines ways of embodying absence on the cyberstage. The spaceless and bodyless character of cyberformance troubles the notion of presence and embodiment, requiring the use of digital tools for the representation of the *real* (i.e., the offline) and for embodying the absence of both performers and spectators. The transformation of the performer's body in cyberspace, as well as the auditorium's absent presence, is discussed, referring to the case of *Cyberian Chalk Circle*, where UpStage, Facebook and Second Life turned into meeting points for distant people to connect and share stories.

In CCC1 and CCC2, Grusha's presence was marked through the polymorphic space of the cyberstage. The chat box, the webcam avatar and the computer-generated voice all played a crucial role for the embodiment of the character on stage. The webcam allows cyberformers to frame specific parts of their face and body and hide other parts in a cinematic way. Despite the fragmental character of the framed doubles, the audience gets a complete idea of the body-flesh of the character/performer by connecting those images. The tableau aesthetics of the montaged body image – the fragmented body – creates a polymorphic space that allows audience disengagement and, thus, critical participation. In CCC1's

DOI: 10.1057/9781137577047.0007

introduction, the text box was used to cover half of Grusha's face (Figure 3.4) to experiment and play with the idea of 'framing'. In *CCC1* (Act I) and *CCC2* (Part B), the audience could see the whole face of Grusha, as well as parts of her body, as framed by the webcam (Figure 3.5).

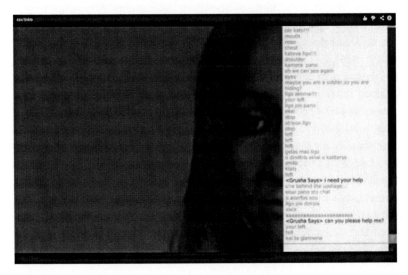

**FIGURE 3.4**    *Screenshot showing Grusha's half-covered face (CCC1, Introduction, 05:54 min).*

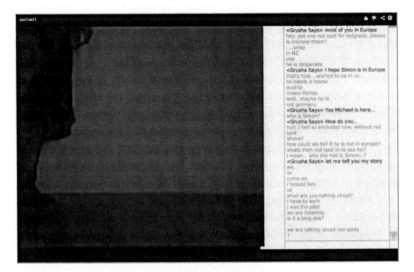

**FIGURE 3.5**    *Screenshot showing Grusha's fragmented body (CCC1, Act I, 00:51 min).*

DOI: 10.1057/9781137577047.0007

However, the audience had no direct image of the performer's eyes, the so-called mirror of the soul, in CCC1 or CCC2 for two reasons. First, it was not technically possible for Stamatiou to look towards the camera at the same time as she tracked the chat box and responded to audience comments. Second, the aim was to comment on the face capture of a webcam, where the object looks at its double instead of the camera filming it. Cyberculture has been continuously accused of making the *representation* of an event more important than the event itself. This can be considered as a form of *Gestus*, the embodiment of the social behaviour of computer users as expressed by their physical gestures through the position of the eyes' gaze.

In CCC3, Grusha's presence became *tele*-present. Here the connection was 'normal', as webcasting was used, and the audience could clearly see and hear Grusha, who responded verbally to their comments in the chat box. This allowed some sort of freedom to the performer to play with the webcam and look towards the camera in moments of tension or come closer and whisper, for instance, that is, act in a more cinematic way. When Grusha wanted to say something to Simon secretly, she used the text box so that no one could hear her, adapting theatrical conventions in cyberformance. The presence of Grusha in the text box was crucial in CCC3 for creating a sense of co-presence among the audience, as she mainly used a different tool from that of the participants to communicate with them. Cyberformance directors need to adapt new conventions of performance for online theatre, as new creative tools are present on the cyberstage.

Apart from the webcam pictures and the chat box, the UpStage drawing tool was used for plot development in CCC1 (Act II), through which Michael's presence was marked. The real-time drawings, based on simple lines similar to a child's sketches, aimed to emphasize Michael's absent presence (Figure 3.6). The 'no body, no eyes, no mouth, no stomach' simple sketches reinforced the V-effect, as the audience gave its own interpretation to the abstract drawings. Someone commented that Michael looked like a 'black star', triggering someone else to ask 'why he is a "black star" to you?', in the search for symbolic meanings (Papagiannouli, 2013a).

Pictures related to the Egyptian rebellion were used as backgrounds (backdrops) for narrating the revolution, while the sound of 'white noise' represented the chaotic sounds of the real riots, forming in this way political memories of Tahrir Square. In CCC1 the backdrops focused

DOI: 10.1057/9781137577047.0007

**FIGURE 3.6**    *Screenshot showing simple line drawings representing Grusha and Michael (CCC1, Act II, 09:49 min).*

on the political usage of the Internet as used by the Egyptians, whereas in *CCC2* these focused on the similarities between World War I and the revolution in Egypt. Apart from space memories, sounds were used to frame the character of Michael: I used the playful sound of water drops in *CCC2* and the sound of a baby's cry in *CCC3*. Although the backdrops and the sounds are pre-captured materials, their presence in cyberformance is important for successful communication with the audience. According to Law (2003), because English is the network language, the use of images is essential for communicating political ideas to non-English-speaking Internet users:

> The capacity to express oneself in a foreign language is not a simple task, however, particularly when communicating political ideas. As a result photos, usually complete with captions in English, have become a new lingua franca of communication. [ ... ] (Law, 2003, p. 243)

> These conversations and photos help to shape political spaces that exist in symbiotic relation to the real, and bring new voices and perspectives to ongoing issues that can be discussed further at face-to-face meetings. (Law, 2003, p. 249)

Language is a key feature in the Etheatre Project for communication between the performance (performers) and spectators because of its text-based character. This is obvious particularly in *CCC1*, where most of

DOI: 10.1057/9781137577047.0007

the audience members were Greek – Stamatiou and I are Greek, and we used our Facebook and Twitter accounts to advertise the performance. As a result, a significant proportion of the audience text was typed in Greeklish – the Greek language written using Latin alphabets. However, in order to play and participate actively, the participants soon began chatting in English, as Grusha did not reply to any Greek message. During the audience discussion after the performance, some participants complained about not being able to type in Greek and discussed the devastation of the Greek language, a major socio-political topic in Greece. The use of the foreign language in CCC1 broke the fourth wall for the Greek audience, as they had to use a language different from their own to engage with the performance; this also did not allow emotional engagement with the story. The foreign-language distancing effect ('L-effect') in such an international event is very important in relation to the politics of engagement in political cyberformance.

Participation is key in cyberformance for creating the notion of presence (or co-presence). According to Fewster (2010a), in digital media, presence is defined by participation. To warm up the audience and prepare them for participating actively in the performance, I began each show with an introductory act. Audience warm-up is essential in an interactive performance as it is the overall atmosphere that 'get[s] people in the mood to participate' (Grindstaff, 2002, p. 122). In CCC1, Grusha introduced herself and her story and asked the participants to locate themselves. Following audience answers, red spots were added on a world atlas to map participants' locations. Ideally, the audience would be able to spot themselves on the map; however, this was not possible on UpStage at the time of the performance. Hence, the map exercise became a challenging geographical game. When unsure about a place, the audience's help was sought to assist in locating them by giving further information.

I arrived at this warm-up exercise by imitating online map tools that automatically map the number and the location of the visitors to a website to create a communal experience. These tools give the sense of co-presence to visitors, who at any time know how many people and from which part of the globe are sharing the same information space with them. In the 'map scene', audience presence was marked through the chat box in which participants typed in their own interpretation of the mapping, connecting the red dots to blood spots and correlating the outcome to a journey. Moreover, although not pre-planned, the audience

DOI: 10.1057/9781137577047.0007

also helped Grusha to fit her webcam on the UpStage platform. Here, the technical weakness of accurately fitting the webcam avatar on stage motivated the spectators to interact: they either described what they *saw*, such as 'nose' and 'mouth', or urged the performer to go 'left' and 'up'.

To push the show in terms of audience interaction in a cross-platform experience, the audience were asked to become the intermediary between Grusha and Simon and help them connect. Grusha was unable to use Google, Facebook or Twitter to locate Simon, owing to Egyptian government restrictions at that time. In *CCC1* (Act III) and *CCC2* (Act II), Grusha asked the audience to help her find Simon and explain to him why she had to marry someone else. Most audience members found Simon on Facebook and contacted him either by posting on his wall or by sending him a personal message. The participants who did not find Simon on Facebook enriched the cyberformance experience by advocating their own findings, such as playing Ralph H. Baer and Howard J. Morrison's electronic memory game called 'Simon' (applied in *CCC1*).

I had pre-created Simon's Facebook account, adding information regarding his work and hometown, messages to Grusha and videos related to the revolution in Egypt. I also used a series of personal photographs of Tsinikoris to portray Simon in different places in the world, so the audience would be unable to locate him. Following the aesthetics of the photographs, which depicted the back of the performer in different well-known sights, such as the Parthenon in Athens, an additional picture was shot with Simon searching for Grusha.

Ironically, to be ethically correct, fake Facebook accounts had to be created for the audience to use. Although this is unethical by Facebook policies, in terms of academic ethics the participants' Facebook accounts had to be protected. To incorporate the fake accounts in the performance, a *CCC1* participant comment was used claiming that Facebook provides data to national intelligence agencies in the United States (see Papagiannouli, 2013b). Furthermore, each Facebook account included information related to the performance. One of the accounts, for instance, linked to the 'We Are All Khaled Said' Facebook group.

Both UpStage and Waterwheel Tap stages count the number of computers linked to the platform, giving a sense of audience existence in the theatrical setting. However, as discussed earlier, audience presence was marked mainly through the chat box, a text-based communication space where the audience could share, exchange, question and interact

DOI: 10.1057/9781137577047.0007

with the performance. Participants described what they saw ('Men can stop a tank'), shared their feelings ('I am shocked'), made personal connections ('My sister is a professor of Egyptology'), gave their interpretation of the performance ('Milk – mothers comfort [...] marriage is a form of slavery') and criticized other audience members ('Maybe one person who is making fun of it but there are more of us here').

Text-based communication is crucial in cyberformance in terms of co-presence, not only for the audience but also for the performers, in the sense of the inevitable participation of spectator presence on stage (Lehmann, 2006, pp. 141–42; Fewster, 2010, p. 46). Like the classic theatre experience, the presence of an audience is fundamental for the *magic* of theatre. The chat box serves to replace the spectators' shadows in the auditorium. In CCC2, audience existence was also marked through Second Life avatars. The avatars, as virtual puppets of the participants, watched the performance through the virtual stage created on Second Life for the festival.

Drawing mainly on the *Cyberian Chalk Circle* project, this chapter completes an account of the practical work of the Etheatre Project research. The success of Etheatre lies in its collaboration with external artists and platforms and the political and dialectical participation of audiences in the performances. Although the number of connected computers did not exceed 30 in each performance, the Etheatre Project participants engaged politically with the performance responding effectively to discussion topics. In cyberformances, audience size cannot be accurately measured as it is not known how many participants are behind the same connected computer. Etheatre performances, for instance, were also streamed in offline venues round the world as part of UpStage Festivals, including in schools in New Zealand and the New Zealand Film Archive, the Govett Brewster Gallery (New Zealand), the Amherst College (Massachusetts), the Marionet Theatro (Portugal), the Piet Zwart Institute and the MAD Emerging Art Centre (Netherlands), the APO33 (France), the Galerija Elektrika (Serbia), the Bikeshed Theatre (UK), the Werkstatt am Hauptplatz in partnership with Kunstraum Goethestrasse (Austria), Signalraum (Germany) and the 19 Tory Street Art Space (New Zealand). The Etheatre Project effectuates the Brechtian theory of political performance for the age of the Internet, turning the cyberstage into a dialectical, in-between space for cyber-collaboration between the audience and the performers and among the performers themselves.

DOI: 10.1057/9781137577047.0007

# Notes

1   According to Susan Sontag and Paul Willemen, the 'perfect spectator' prefers
    to sit in the third row at the centre (cited in De Valck, 2007, p. 182), a notion
    that allows cinema and theatre directors to stage productions in accordance
    with the perfect spectator's view.

2   Available at: https://docs.google.com/spreadsheet/viewform?formkey=dFI1V3
    RabFYwVHk3LWMzVnpzU3JCZUE6MQ

3   In response to the questions 'How did you find out about the boy's murder?'
    and 'What did you do after 6 December 2008?' (*Merry Crisis and a Happy New
    Fear*, 2012).

DOI: 10.1057/9781137577047.0007

# Conclusion: Political Cyberformance. Past or Future?

Abstract: *The conclusion summarizes the research findings determined through the practice-based methodologies of the Etheatre Project, not only presenting answers to questions Papagiannouli raises at the start of this book but also raising questions that need further investigation to reveal the future of cyberformance. Political cyberformance, by allowing the democratic interaction and conflictual participation of the audience in the formation and realization of a theatrical performance, forms political spaces through performance on the cyberstage. This is important for the presence of theatre in cyberspace because it considers how audiences are presented within new dialectical performance environments and measures the impact of these interactive relationships with regard to the political response of spectators in real time during a performance.*

Papagiannouli, Christina. *Political Cyberformance: The Etheatre Project*. Basingstoke: Palgrave Macmillan, 2016. DOI: 10.1057/ 9781137577047.0008.

The aim of the study was to examine the political and participative character of cyberformance under the umbrella of Brecht's political theatre. Cyberformance gives rise to the idea of a new Brechtian relationship between the stage and the audience, by offering tools for real-time audience interaction and feedback. The polymorphic in-between space of the cyberstage allows co-creation between artists and the audience distributed in cyberspace through devices for real-time collaboration and participation.

A brief overview of the historical development of cyberformance, in the context of present-day examples of the use of the Internet in leading art houses and theatre companies, highlighted the new wave of UK-based theatre 'cyber turn'. The introductory section in Chapter 1 looked at the RSC's *Such Tweet Sorrow* in relation to earlier examples of Shakespearian cyber-adaptations, including the Hamnet Players' productions, concluding that not much difference exists in the theatrical use of online platforms from #Hamnet to #Dream40 performances. However, the CyPosium and the 121212 UpStage Festival, both of which examined the history of cyberformance to signify its future and gave rise to new questions and considerations, marked 2012 as the *year of cyberformance*.

Chapter 1 investigated the characteristics of online theatre, looking at cyberformance as the outcome of the intermedial negotiation between theatre and the Internet. Liveness and interactivity were established as the primary attributes of cyberformance, deriving from the live character of theatre and the development of the Internet as an interactive medium. In cyberformance, liveness is no longer an aesthetic choice, but rather a basic trait that is directly connected to the interactive and participative character of the Internet, as without real-time engagement the notion of co-presence is weak and, thus, liveness is meaningless. The critical comparison between Royal National Theatre's NTLive *Phèdre* production and Forced Entertainment's 24-hour *Quizoola!* helped to reinforce the importance of interactivity for creating liveness in online theatre, demonstrating the crucial differences between online theatre and live cinema.

To establish the political character of cyberformance, Chapter 1 also investigated emergent economic, social and political implications and interactions of the Internet with physical space and society, studying the political use of the Internet in Egypt of 2011, the potato revolution in Greece and the Turkish Spring of 2013. These examples draw attention to the growing distance between 'digital' and 'cyber', evident in the clear distinction between controlled government digital media and self-managed public Internet sources, demonstrating the power of the Internet in terms of public participation. However, the risk of the use of the Internet as a surveillance tool and control mechanism exists – an important fact for future political cyberformance directors and practitioners who will need to protect the real identities of the participants.

Chapter 2 explored notions of socio-political engagement in online practices and the importance of social networking platforms in public participation through examples of uses of the Internet in theatre making and staging. The performance review in this chapter locates the Etheatre Project in a lineage of practice, allowing the *practical* study of online theatre boundaries and characteristics. The discussion of the re-democratization of theatre in terms of audience conflictual participation in interactive and participative theatre focused on the case of the NTW Community blog (a radicalized form of national theatre that extends the role of the public in decision making and allows citizens to reclaim theatre as a public good) and the *Radicalisation of Bradley Manning* performance.

I studied the intercultural character of cyberformance with reference to the productions of Verhoeven's *Life Streaming* and Rimini Protokoll's *Call Cutta in a Box*. Both performances used the Internet as a space for cultural exchange, breaking the boundaries of *virtual touch* by developing a degree of intimacy and interaction between performers and audience members and between the distributed spaces in which the performances took place. Verhoeven installed antennas in Sri Lanka to connect distant people to share experiences and comment on media representation of individuals as passive victims, focusing on the case of the 2004 tsunami in Indonesia. On the contrary, Rimini Protokoll used existing technology, which had made India 'become the back office of the western world' (Haug, 2012), to introduce the people behind the voice. An analysis of Abrahams' *Angry Women* and Brager's *You Are Invited* helped to highlight the cyber-collaboration between distributed artists who have not necessarily met face to face. The intermedial use of the Internet in their work turned the computer screen into an intercultural window, connecting distant people, cultures and places. Thus, cyberformance brings community back to its initial purpose – *to commune* (through democratic but critical participation), which Schutzman suggests is 'to talk together, to be in close rapport' (2006, p. 139).

DOI: 10.1057/9781137577047.0008

Chapter 2 also examined different online spaces and the spatial experience caused by public cyberformance. Cases in point included the Høyblokka Project's use of the Internet as a memory archive space, collecting and archiving memories of Trondheim citizens about their city's old hospital building that was demolished during the street performance of the project; Merton and Folds' cyber–street theatre performances on the online public platform of Chatroulette; Jamieson's use of private spaces (e.g., participants' houses) and public spaces (e.g., galleries, libraries and laboratories) to stream eco-cyberformances; and Field Broadcast's nine-day-long virus-like performances that 'infected' the computer screen of the audience with UK-based landscapes.

Chapter 3 discussed the directing methodologies of the Etheatre Project – cyber-adaptation, cyber-ethnotheatre and cyber-collaboration – in the context of Brecht's theories to study the role of the director as 'discussion facilitator' in political cyberformance. Here, political cyberformance refers to the directorial practices of *making cyberformance politically* (in Brechtian terms), rather than cyberformance with political content (see Barnett, 2015, p. 32). In the Etheatre Project, the role of the director is to promote real-time conversation between audience members and performers in a chat box and assist the conflictual/dialectical participation of spectators in the performance, while preserving their anonymity. This is not only to protect the real identities of the participants, but also to release the audience from social masks and decorous behaviour and allow authentic interactions.

The Etheatre Project provided spaces for people to find voice. 'As arenas that are subject to constant negotiation and renegotiation', social-networking platforms turn into political spaces that are 'an active and interactive context in which social relations and structures are transformed over time' (Jones, 2000, cited in Brock, Cornwall and Gaventa, 2001, p. 23). In *Cyberian Chalk Circle*, the audience judged Grusha for getting married, made decisions about Simon's life and debated contemporary socio-political issues, turning UpStage into a political space for real-time adaptation. In *Merry Crisis and a Happy New Fear*, audience members replied to questions in a questionnaire during the performance, taking active part in the co-creation of a real-time verbatim cyberformance in which they became the performers and the witnesses of the represented performative. In *Etheatre Project and Collaborators*, the audience became part of the collective ensemble, sharing personal stories alongside those of the collaborators. These examples demonstrate

DOI: 10.1057/9781137577047.0008

that cyberformance's use of the Internet as a debating space for political expression and participation forms political and dialectical spaces through performance within cyberspace.

In Chapter 3, I also provided a factual and logistical account of the production circumstances, closely looking at the rehearsal process of each project. I discussed my work with professional actress Evi Stamatiou and the use of Stanislavsky's method to reach a balance in the adapted character of Grusha, between the Brechtian play and the Egyptian circumstances of our performance, and build strong connections for *Cyberian Chalk Circle*. We paid great attention to detail, taking into consideration factual information such as the time zone, weather conditions and the exact geographical location of the Egyptian Grusha to answer any questions the audience raised for Grusha via the chat box in the course of the performance. Moreover, I looked at the use of textual improvisation in the chat box as a method to build the narrative of the piece. The improvisational character of the project allowed space for audience interpretation, sharing dialectical thinking and critical participation.

In contrast, the *Merry Crisis and a Happy New Fear* production could not be considered a successful experiment in terms of audience conflictual participation. This was mainly because of the tightness of the script, which, in contrast to the improvisational character of the first project, did not leave room for further discussion, and because of the disrupted communication between audience members (chat box) and performers (webcam/ life streaming), as proved in the *CCC3* open rehearsal. For *Merry Crisis and a Happy New Fear*, I worked with two performers interested in the topic of protest as theatre to create a real-time verbatim performance. We approached the answers collected through a questionnaire in a Brechtian manner, looking at their 'fixed the not-but' character – participants gave different interpretations of the same event, which was reflected in their responses to the questions. We also worked on the rhythm of the verbatim script to prepare performers for incorporating audience text during the actual performance. We used physical movements and streaming effects to create transitional moments and link the different question-based scenes.

Following the unsuccessful experiment of the use of a tight script, *Etheatre Project and Collaborators* was devised as a performance about migration based on improvisational moments, where discussions between performers and spectators took place in the chat box. Here,

DOI: 10.1057/9781137577047.0008

blocked cues functioned as transitional moments to link the improvised discussions and inspire audience reflection on the topic. As I learnt through the Etheatre Project, the work of a cyberformance director in such a completely remote cyber-collaborative production is to manage and facilitate the collaborators, allowing the responses, ideas and needs of collaborating groups to shape the final product. My role as a director and facilitator was tested in my readiness to assist members of the group at any moment, and in my ability to find practical solutions to problems arising during the rehearsal process and in real time during the performance – fundamental responsibilities of a director as facilitator.

The intermedial exchange between theatre and the Internet resulted in a more democratic and interactive approach to theatre directing in terms of radical participation, as proved by the Etheatre Project. The collaborators as well as the audience co-directed the cyberformances by influencing the discussions that took place during real-time improvisational moments. This is noteworthy for future cyberformance research and practice, as cyberformance directors should allow space for such audience interaction and conflictual participation. However, in political cyberformances the existence of a structured performance plan or script is central not only to assisting discussion between performers and audience members but also to ensuring a smooth performance and to providing cues for scene changes. Despite the complexities of a cyberformance – as seen in the final project, where avatars, drawings, sound backdrops and live streaming coexisted on the cyberstage to showcase the range of tools of the cyberstage – a cyberformance director should use cyberstage tools rationally, choosing appropriately the ones that match the needs of each project.

In this monograph, I generated new knowledge for directing political cyberformances by using the Internet exclusively as a performance space for a distributed, anonymous audience to connect and participate actively in political happenings. Despite limitations of a low budget, the Etheatre Project managed to achieve high levels of participation and interaction, by focusing exclusively on online audience members. A large offline audience presence could have been achieved by splitting the concentration of performers in two directions, usually leaving online participants exposed. I argue that the presence of an offline audience can be effective for both online and offline participants only if the company can provide a device (e.g., a computer, a laptop, a smartphone or a tablet) to every offline spectator. Only then can offline and online audience members

DOI: 10.1057/9781137577047.0008

have equal opportunity to participate and communicate. Equality is key in cyberformance, as proved by the 'failure' of *CCC3* and *Merry Crisis and a Happy New Fear* and the study of co-presence on the cyberstage – an important fact for future researchers and practitioners who will deal with updated online tools and platforms. In the Etheatre Project, the chat box thus became the most important part of the cyberstage, where real-time, remote cyber-collaboration between the audience and the performers was allowed to take place.

Some of the topics touched upon here that could be further investigated include scenography, acting and the political body in cyberformance. Cyberformance opens up new possibilities for scenographers to experiment with the empty stage of the Internet and with digital and online tools for real-time set creation, such as the drawing tools that UpStage and Waterwheel Tap offer. Research on cyberformance acting is crucial for studying its intermedial character, an in-between theatrical and cinematic form of acting. The Etheatre Project opened the discussion on the political character of cyberformance, focusing on its dialectic nature. This sets the basis for further research on the physical character of political theatre and the use of *Gestus* in cyberformance.

As with any research on digital performance, questions about the future of cyberformance inevitably emerged at the end of the Etheatre Project too. I am not sure whether a bright future awaits cyberformance, but I can definitely argue that there is a bright present. The 7 million pounds made available by the Digital R&D Fund for the Arts – a partnership between NESTA, the Arts Council England and the Arts and Humanities Research Council – for supporting digital projects and encouraging interdisciplinary collaborations between artists, media experts and researchers between 2012 and 2015 proves present-day interest in digital and online performances and in the UK-based arts' cyber turn. However, I do not believe that this will eliminate classic forms of theatre, as the more we turn to technology the more we search for moments of rest from it. Instead, I argue that cyberformance, the outcome of the intermedial marriage between theatre and the Internet, can remind theatre that its main characteristic is the live communication between performers and audience members and can stimulate the Internet to build its own aesthetics and promote creativity. What remains is to see what the future holds for cyberformance, both politically and artistically.

DOI: 10.1057/9781137577047.0008

# Bibliography

Abrahams, A. (2011a) Interviewed by Evi Tsirigotaki for 'Simeio Art'. *Greek Public Television NET*. Available at: http://aabrahams.wordpress.com/tag/eve-tsirigotaki/; https://www.youtube.com/watch?v=0eE36dwhLgg (Both accessed: 31 January 2013).

Abrahams, A. (2011b) 'Trapped to reveal: on webcam mediated communication and collaboration'. *Journal for Artistic Research*. Available at: http://www.researchcatalogue.net/view/18236/18237 (Accessed: 11 June 2013).

Abrahams, A. (2011–12) *Angry Women: An Artistic Research Project*. Available at: http://www.bram.org/angry/women/ (Accessed: 17 January 2014).

Abrahams, A. (2012) Interviewed by Christina Papagiannouli. 30 November. Available at: http://etheatre.info/e_theatre/Annie_Abrahams.html (Accessed: 16 January 2014).

Adams, M., Ball, M., Robertson, M., Thornbury, S. and Tims, C. (2010) 'The digital democracy'. *The LIFT Talks*, 24 June. Available at: http://www.liftfest.com/events/past-events/2010-lift-festival/the-lift-talks (Accessed: 15 January 2014).

Andrews, B. (2001) 'Brechtian V-effect updated: implications for poetic praxis'. *Crayon*, 3, pp. 1–12. Available at: http://fordhamenglish.squarespace.com/storage/Bruce%20Andrews%2022Brechtian%20V-Effect%20Updated22.pdf (Accessed: 19 January 2014).

Anstey, J. (2007) 'Theater and virtual reality'. *Noema, Special Section on Drama, Performance and Digital Multimedia*,

DOI: 10.1057/9781137577047.0009

*19th Cairo International Festival for Experimental Theater, Special Arts.*
Available at: http://org.noemalab.eu/sections/specials/cairo_drama_
conference/Anstey_Cairo.pdf (Accessed: 26 January 2013).

Anywhere (2013) Available at: http://anywherefest.com/ (Accessed:
18 January 2014).

Aristotle (1981) [1962] *The Politics.* Translated by T. A. Sinclair. Revised
and re-presented by Trevor J. Saunders. Penguin Classics Series.
Middlesex: Penguin.

Artaud, A. (1958) [1938] *The Theater and Its Double.* Translated by Mary
Caroline Richards. New York: Grove Weidenfeld.

Arts and Humanities Research Council. (2012) 'Funding opportunities:
digital research & development fund for the arts'. *Arts and Humanities
Research Council.* Available at: http://www.ahrc.ac.uk/Funding-
Opportunities/Pages/Digital-Research-Development-Fund-for-the-
Arts.aspx (Accessed: 9 January 2014).

Arts Council England (2012) *Annual Review 2010/11.* London: The
Stationery Office. Available at: http://www.artscouncil.org.uk/
media/uploads/pdf/ACEannual_review201011_Accessible_PDF.pdf
(Accessed: 9 June 2013).

Ashcroft, B., Griffiths, G. and Tiffin, H. (2002) *The Empire Writes Back:
Theory and Practice in Post-Colonial Literatures*, 2nd edn. London and
New York: Routledge.

Auslander, P. (1999) *Liveness: Performance in a Mediatized Culture.* Oxon,
UK: Routledge.

Bakhshi, H. and Throsby, D. (2010) 'Culture of innovation: an economic
analysis of innovation in arts and cultural organisations'. *NESTA
Research Report*, 10 June. London: NESTA. Available at: http://www.
nesta.org.uk/sites/default/files/culture_of_innovation.pdf (Accessed:
9 January 2014).

Bakhtin, M. (1981) *The Dialogic Imagination: Four Essays.* Edited by
M. Holquist. Translated by C. Emerson and M. Holquist. Austin:
University of Texas Press.

Ball, M. (2013) 'Digital futures: "It's the network, stupid" '. *The Guardian*,
19 February. Available at: http://www.theguardian.com/culture-
professionals-network/culture-professionals-blog/2013/feb/19/
clore-essays-digital-arts-network (Accessed: 9 October 2013).

Ban Ki-moon (2013) '[Message for] International Migrants Day:
18 December'. *United Nations.* Available at: http://www.un.org/en/
events/migrantsday/ (Accessed: 9 July 2014).

DOI: 10.1057/9781137577047.0009

Barnett, D. (2011) 'Undogmatic Marxism: Brecht rehearses at the Berliner', in Bradley, L. and Leeder, K. (eds) *Brecht and the GDR: Politics, Culture, Posterity*. Edinburgh German Yearbook: Volume 5. Rochester and New York: Camden House, pp. 25–44.

Barnett, D. (2012) 'Dusting off a lively corpse: excavating Brecht the director from the archive'. *TaPRA Directing and Dramaturgy Working Group Paper, TaPRA 2012 Conference*, 6 September. Canterbury: University of Kent. Abstract available at: http://tapra.org/category/news-calls/tapra-conference-2012/ (Accessed: 19 January 2014).

Barnett, D. (2013) 'The Berliner Ensemble: Bertolt Brecht's theories of theatrical collaboration as practice', in Britton, J. (ed.) *Encountering Ensemble*. London and New York: Bloomsbury Methuen Drama, pp. 126–141.

Barnett, D. (2015) *Brecht in Practice: Theatre, Theory and Performance*. London and New York: Bloomsbury Methuen Drama Engage.

Beardshaw, T. (2012) 'The next step to social networking is building your own online community'. *The Guardian*, 18 January. Available at: http://www.theguardian.com/culture-professionals-network/culture-professionals-blog/2012/jan/18/social-network-arts-wales-theatre (Accessed: 8 October 2013).

Beaudry, J. and El Baroni, B. (2010) 'Postscript', in Miessen, M., *The Nightmare of Participation (Crossbench Praxis as a Mode of Criticality)*. Berlin: Sternberg Press, pp. 253–256. Available at: http://www.boxwith.com/2010/11/02/a-postscript-to-the-nightmare-of-participation/ (Accessed: 4 January 2014).

Beckley, R. (1962) 'Adaptation as a feature of Brecht's dramatic technique'. *German Life and Letters*, 15(4), pp. 274–284.

Bennett, J. and Kennedy, R. (2003) 'Introduction', in Bennett, J. and Kennedy, R. (eds) *World Memory: Personal Trajectories in Global Time*. Hampshire: Palgrave Macmillan, pp. 1–15.

Bhabha, H. K. (1995) 'Cultural diversity and cultural differences', in Ashcroft, B., Griffiths, G. and Tiffin, H. (eds) *The Post-Colonial Studies Reader*. London and New York: Routledge, pp. 155–157. Available at: http://www.everydayarchive.org/art500/wp-content/uploads/2011/08/bhabha_cultural-diversity.pdf (Accessed: 20 January 2014).

Bishop, C. (2006) 'The social turn: collaboration and its discontents'. *Artforum*, February, pp. 178–183. Available at: http://www.gc.cuny.edu/CUNY_GC/media/CUNY-Graduate-Center/PDF/Art%20History/Claire%20Bishop/Social-Turn.pdf (Accessed: 18 January 2014).

Bishop, C. (2012) *Artificial Hells: Participatory Art and the Politics of Spectatorship*. New York: Verso.

Blandford, S. (2013) 'Introduction', in Blandford, S. (ed.) *Theatre & Performance in Small Nations*. Bristol: Intellect Ltd., pp. 1–18.

Blast Theory (2014) 'Our history and approach'. *Blast Theory*. Available at: http://www.blasttheory.co.uk/our-history-approach/ (Accessed: 11 January 2014).

Bolter, J. D. and Grusin, R. (2000) *Remediation: Understanding New Media*. Cambridge, MA: MIT Press.

Bradley, L. (2006) *Brecht and Political Theatre: The Mother on Stage*. Oxford, UK: Clarendon Press.

Brager, Ø. U. (2012) Interviewed by Christina Papagiannouli. 29 April. Available at: http://etheatre.info/e_theatre/ystein_Ulsberg_Brager. html (Accessed: 16 January 2014).

Brecht, B. (1930) *He Said Yes / He Said No*. Digitalized by RevSocialist for SocialistStories. Available at: http://socialiststories.net/liberate/ He%20Said%20Yes,%20He%20Said%20No%20-%20Bertolt%20 Brecht.pdf (Accessed: 20 January 2014).

Brecht, B. (1964a) [1932] 'An example of pedagogics', in Willett, J. (ed. and transl.) *Brecht on Theatre: The Development of an Aesthetic*. New York: Hill and Wang, pp. 31–32.

Brecht, B. (1964b) [1932] 'The radio as an apparatus of communication', in Willett, J. (ed. and transl.) *Brecht on Theatre: The Development of an Aesthetic*. New York: Hill and Wang, pp. 51–52.

Brecht, B. (1964c) [1933] 'New technique of acting', in Willett, J. (ed. and transl.) *Brecht on Theatre: The Development of an Aesthetic*. New York: Hill and Wang, pp. 136–147.

Brecht, B. (1964d) [1949] 'A short organum for the theatre', in Willett, J. (ed. and transl.) *Brecht on Theatre: The Development of an Aesthetic*. New York: Hill and Wang, pp. 179–208.

Broadhurst, S. (2007) *Digital Practices: Aesthetic and Neuroaesthetic Approaches to Performance and Technology*. New York: Palgrave Macmillan.

Brock, K., Cornwall, A. and Gaventa, J. (2001) 'Power, knowledge and political spaces in the framing of poverty policy'. *IDS Working Paper 143*. Sussex: Institute of Development Studies (IDS). Available at: http://www.ids.ac.uk/idspublication/power-knowledge-and-political-spaces-in-the-framing-of-poverty-policy (Accessed: 5 December 2011).

DOI: 10.1057/9781137577047.0009

Brook, P. (1996) 'Peter Brook', in Delgado, M. M. and Heritage, P. (eds) *In Contact with the Gods?: Directors Talk Theatre*. Manchester and New York: Manchester University Press, pp. 36–54.

Cardwell, S. (2002) *Adaptation Revisited: Television and the Classic Novel*. Manchester and New York: Manchester University Press.

Carney, S. (2005) *Brecht and Critical Theory: Dialectics and Contemporary Aesthetics*. Oxon and New York: Routledge.

Carpentier, N. and Cammaerts, B. (2006) 'Hegemony, democracy, agonism and journalism: an interview with Chantal Mouffe'. *Journalism Studies*, 7(6), pp. 964–975 (PDF pp. 1–14). Available at: http://eprints.lse.ac.uk/3020/; http://eprints.lse.ac.uk/3020/1/Hegemony%2C_democracy%2C_agonism_and_journalism_%28LSERO%29.pdf (Accessed: 22 November 2013).

Cartledge, P. (1997) '"Deep plays": theatre as process in Greek civil life', in Easterling, P. E. (ed.) *The Cambridge Companion to Greek Tragedy*. Cambridge: Cambridge University Press, pp. 3–35.

Case, S. E. (2007) 'Digital divas: sex and gender in cyberspace', in Detsi-Diamanti, Z., Kitsi-Mitakou, K. and Yiannopoulou, E. (eds) *The Flesh Made Text Made Flesh: Cultural and Theoretical Returns to the Body*. New York: Peter Lang, pp. 27–42.

Causey, M. (2003) 'Cyber-theatre', in Kennedy, D. (ed.) *Oxford Encyclopedia of Theatre & Performance A–L*, vol. 1. Oxford, UK: Oxford University Press, p. 341.

Causey, M. (2006) *Theatre and Performance in Digital Culture: From Simulation to Embeddedness*. London and New York: Routledge.

Cavendish, D. (2010) 'All the world's a digital stage'. *The Telegraph*, 1 June. Available at: http://www.telegraph.co.uk/culture/theatre/theatre-features/7793492/All-the-worlds-adigital-stage.html (Accessed: 24 June 2011).

Centre Régional D'Art Contemporain Languedoc-Roussillon (2011–12) *Training for a Better World – Annie Abrahams*. Available at: http://crac.languedocroussillon.fr/exposition_fiche/121/3171-archives-expositions-art-contemporain.htm (Accessed: 17 January 2014).

Chapple, F. and Kattenbelt, C. (2006) 'Key issues in intermediality in theatre and performance', in Chapple, F. and Kattenbelt, C. (eds) *Intermediality in Theatre and Performance*. Amsterdam: Rodopi, pp. 11–25.

Chatroulette (2009) Available at: http://chatroulette.com/ (Accessed: 18 January 2014).

DOI: 10.1057/9781137577047.0009

Chatzichristodoulou, M. (2006) 'Cyber theaters: emergent, hybrid, networked performance practices'. *Sklunk*. Available at: http://www. sklunk.net/cybertheaters (Accessed: 5 December 2010).

Chatzichristodoulou, M. (2010) *Cybertheatres: Emergent Networked Performance Practices*. Unpublished PhD Thesis. London: Goldsmiths College, University of London.

Chatzichristodoulou, M. (2012) 'Cyberformance? Digital or networked performance? Cybertheaters? Or virtual theatres?... Or all of the above?' *CyPosium: Cyberformance Symposium*. 12 October. Available at: http://www.cyposium.net/selected-presentations/ chatzichristodoulou/ (Accessed: 26 January 2013).

Chatzichristodoulou, M. (2014) 'Cyberformance? Digital or networked performance? Cybertheaters? Or virtual theatres?... Or all of the above?', in Abrahams A. and Jamieson, H. V. (eds) *Cyposium – the Book*. Brescia: Link Editions, pp. 19–30.

Cohen-Cruz, J. (1998) *Radical Street Performance: An International Anthology*. Oxon and New York: Routledge.

Collinge, G. (2011) 'All about *Such Tweet Sorrow*'. *Digital Content Development Programme*. 24 February. Available at: http://www. dcdprogramme.org.uk/projects/projects/such-tweet-sorrow/ (Accessed: 20 May 2013).

Curtis, R. (2013) '*Quizoola!* live webcast: #quizoola24'. Forced *Entertainment*, 13 April. Available at: http://www.forcedentertainment. com/page/3104/QUIZOOLA-Live-Webcast (Accessed: 20 November 2013).

*Cyberian Chalk Circle Part A* (2011) Directed by Christina Papagiannouli. 11:11:11 UpStage Festival, UpStage. Performance log Part A 11/11/11. Available at: http://www.etheatre.info/e_theatre/CCCLogA.html (Accessed: 19 January 2014).

*Cyberian Chalk Circle Part B* (2011) Directed by Christina Papagiannouli. 11:11:11 UpStage Festival, UpStage. Performance log Part B 11/11/11. Available at: http://www.etheatre.info/e_theatre/CCCLogB.html (Accessed: 19 January 2014).

*Cyberian Chalk Circle III* (2012) Directed by Christina Papagiannouli. 12:12:12 UpStage Festival, Waterwheel Tap. Performance log CCC3 03/11/12. Available at: http://www.etheatre.info/e_theatre/CCCLog3. html (Accessed: 28 January 2014).

CyPosium (2012) *CyPosium: An Online Symposium on Cyberperformance*. Available at: http://www.cyposium.net/ (Accessed: 4 January 2014).

DOI: 10.1057/9781137577047.0009

Dahlberg, L. and Siapera, E. (2007) 'Introduction: tracing radical democracy and the Internet', in Dahlberg, L. and Siapera, E. (eds) *Radical Democracy and the Internet: Interrogating Theory and Practice*. Hampshire and New York: Palgrave Macmillan, pp. 1–16. Available at: http://www.palgrave.com/pdfs/0230007201.pdf (Accessed: 16 January 2014).

Danet, B. (2002) 'Studies of cyberpl@y: ethical and methodological aspects'. *Working Paper*. Israel: Hebrew University of Jerusalem. Available at: http://citeseerx.ist.psu.edu/viewdoc/download?doi=10.1.1.123.8049&rep=rep1&type=pdf (Accessed: 2 January 2014).

Danet, B., Bechar-Israeli, T., Cividalli, A. and Rosenbaum-Tamari, Y. (2006) 'Curtain time 20:00 GMT: experiments with virtual theater on Internet Relay Chat'. *Journal of Computer-Mediated Communication*, 1(2), section 1.1, para 4. Available at: http://onlinelibrary.wiley.com/doi/10.1111/j.1083-6101.1995.tb00326.x/full (Accessed: 15 May 2013).

Darras, G., Patrelakis, N., Giannakidis, K., Efimeros, K., Tsimitakis, M. and Damatopoulos, S. (2013) 'New media and new journalism'. *ERT (Open)*, 26 June. Available at: http://www.ertopen.com/eidiseis/item/690#.UlgbsWTwJXA (Accessed: 26 June 2013).

De Valck, M. (2007) *Film Festivals: From European Geopolitics to Global Cinephilia*. Amsterdam: Amsterdam University Press. Available at: http://www.scifilondontv.com/FFA/globalff/FilmFestivalsGlobal.pdf (Accessed: 19 January 2014).

De Wend Fenton, R. and Neal, L. (2005) *The Turning World: Stories from the London International Festival of Theatre*. London: Calouste Gulbenkian Foundation.

Derrida, J. (1995) *Archive Fever: A Freudian Impression*. Translated by Eric Prenowitz. Chicago and London: University of Chicago Press. Also published with the same title in *Diacritics*, 25(2), pp. 9–63. Available at: http://beforebefore.net/149a/w11/media/Derrida-Archive_Fever_A_Freudian_Impression.pdf (Accessed: 18 January 2014).

Desktop Theater (2000) Available at: http://www.desktoptheater.org/ (Accessed: 14 January 2014).

Dixon, S. (2003) 'Absent fiends: Internet theatre, posthuman bodies and the interactive void'. *Performance Arts International*. Available at: http://www.robat.scl.net/content/PaiPres/presencesite/html/dixon00.html; https://eprints.mdx.ac.uk/3074/1/html/dixchamel.html (Both accessed: 8 November 2011).

DOI: 10.1057/9781137577047.0009

Dixon, S. (2004) 'Adventures in cyber-theatre (or the actor's fear of the disembodied audience)', in Zapp A. (ed.) *Networked Narrative Environments: As Imaginary Spaces of Being*. Manchester, UK: Manchester Metropolitan University, pp. 99–121.

Dixon, S. (2006) 'Uncanny interactions'. *Performance Research: A Journal of the Performing Arts*, 11(4), pp. 67–75.

Dixon, S. (with contributions by B. Smith) (2007) *Digital Performance: A History of New Media in Theater, Dance, Performance Art, and Installation*. Cambridge, MA: MIT Press.

Doherty, B. (2000) 'Test and *Gestus* in Brecht and Benjamin'. *Modern Language Notes*, 115(3), pp. 442–481.

Eddershaw, M. (1996) *Performing Brecht: Forty Years of British Performances*. London and New York: Routledge.

Eisenbarth, M. (2012) 'A vision for DownStage'. *Foorbarlab: Random Thoughts on Arts, Coding and Open Source*. 8 February. Available at: http://www.foobarlab.net/blog/2012/02/a-vision-for-downstage (Accessed: 2 January 2014).

Ellis, J. (1982) 'The literary adaptation: an introduction'. *Screen*, 23(1), pp. 3–5.

English, J. F. (1994) *Comic Transactions: Literature, Humor, and the Politics of Community in Twentieth-Century Britain*. London and New York: Cornell University Press.

eTV (2013) *Who Is eTV*. Available at: https://www.etv.org.nz/v4/aboutetv.php (Accessed: 4 January 2014).

European Cultural Foundation (2013) 'We have a situation!: Fostering active citizenship through creative networked collaboration'. *ECF Green Paper*. Available at: http://www.wehaveasituation.net/wp-content/uploads/2013/10/greenpaper-1.pdf (Accessed: 11 February 2014).

Feral, J. (1996) 'There are at least three Americas', in Pavis, P. (ed.) *The Intercultural Performance Reader*. Oxon and New York: Routledge, pp. 51–62.

Fewster, R. (2010a) 'Presence', in Bay-Cheng, S., Kattenbelt, C., Lavender, A. and Nelson, R. (eds) *Mapping Intermediality in Performance*. Amsterdam: Amsterdam University Press, pp. 46–47.

Fewster, R. (2010b) 'Instance: *The Lost Babylon* (Adelaide Fringe Festival 2006)', in Bay-Cheng, S., Kattenbelt, C., Lavender, A. and Nelson, R. (eds) *Mapping Intermediality in Performance*. Amsterdam: Amsterdam University Press, pp. 63–68.

Field Broadcast (2010) *About Field Broadcast*. Available at: http://www.fieldbroadcast.org/about.html (Accessed: 16 October 2011).

DOI: 10.1057/9781137577047.0009

Fischlin, D. (2007) 'Virtual Shakespeares: theatrical adaptations and transformations of Shakespeare, 1600–1997'. *Canadian Adaptations of Shakespeare Project*. Available at: http://www. canadianshakespeares.ca/folio/Sources/Virtual_Shakespeares.pdf (Accessed: 18 September 2013).

Forced Entertainment (2013) *#Quizoola24*. 17 May. Available at: http:// notebook.forcedentertainment.com/?p=772 (Accessed: 25 June 2013).

Freshwater, H. (2009) *Theatre & Audience*. Foreword by Lois Weaver. New York: Macmillan.

Fuks, S. (2011) 'World of water. Keith Gallasch: interview, Suzon Fuks, Waterwheel'. *RealTime*, 104, p. 42. Available at: http://www. realtimearts.net/article/issue104/10395 (Accessed: 4 January 2014).

Gardner, L. (2009) 'Rimini Protokoll's theatre of journalism'. *The Guardian*, 7 May. Available at: http://www.theguardian.com/ stage/2009/may/07/rimini-protokoll-theatre-journalism (Accessed: 6 December 2013).

Giannachi, G. (2004) *Virtual Theatres: An Introduction*. London and New York: Routledge.

Giannachi, G. (2007) *The Politics of New Media Theatre: Life*(TM)*. Oxon and New York: Routledge.

GiaNtakos (2008) *Cops Shooting at Alexis Grigoropoulos and Other People (6/12/2008)*. Available at: http://www.youtube.com/ watch?v=jwJZHcMolUA (Accessed: 10 October 2012).

Goldhill, S. (1997) 'The audience of Athenian tragedy', in Easterling, P. E. (ed.) *The Cambridge Companion to Greek Tragedy*. Cambridge: Cambridge University Press, pp. 54–68.

Goleby, L. (2012) 'Streaming out for digital audiences 2'. *Seminar on Live Streaming*, Lighthouse, Brighton, 21 November. Available at: http:// www.lighthouse.org.uk/programme/streaming-out-for-digital-audiences-2 (Accessed: 21 January 2014).

Govan, E., Nickolson, H. and Normington, K. (2007) *Making a Performance: Devising Histories and Contemporary Practices*. London and New York: Routledge.

Green J., Thorington H. and Riel, M. (2004) *Networked_Performance*. Available at: http://turbulence.org/blog/; http://turbulence.org/blog/about/ (Both accessed: 26 January 2013).

Green, J. R. (1994) *Theatre in Ancient Greek Society*. New York: Routledge.

Grindstaff, L. (2002) *The Money Shot: Trash, Class, and the Making of TV Talk Shows*. Chicago and London: University of Chicago Press.

DOI: 10.1057/9781137577047.0009

Grotowski, J. (2002) [1967] 'Towards a poor theatre', in Barba, E. (ed.) *Towards a Poor Theatre: Jerzy Grotowski.* New York: Routledge, pp. 15–26.

Hammond, W. and Steward, D. (2008) 'David Hare & Max Stafford-Clark' [interview], in Hammond, W. and Steward, D. (eds) *Verbatim Verbatim: Contemporary Documentary Theatre.* London: Oberon Books, pp. 45–76.

Haug, H. (2012) Interviewed by Christina Papagiannouli. 30 October. Available at: http://etheatre.info/e_theatre/Helgard_Haug.html (Accessed: 17 January 2014).

Henley, J. (2012) 'Greece on the breadline: "potato movement" links shoppers and farmers'. *The Guardian,* 18 March. Available at: http://www.theguardian.com/world/blog/2012/mar/18/greece-breadline-potato-movement-farmers (Accessed: 6 January 2014).

Howard, P. N., Duffy, A., Freelon, D., Hussain, M., Mari, W. and Mazaid, M. (2011) 'Opening closed regimes: what was the role of social media during the Arab Spring?'. Working Paper 2011.1. Seattle: PIPTI. Available at: http://pitpi.org/index.php/2011/09/11/opening-closed-regimes-what-was-the-role-of-social-media-during-the-arab-spring/; http://pitpi.org/wp-content/uploads/2013/02/2011_Howard-Duffy-Freelon-Hussain-Mari-Mazaid_pITPI.pdf (Accessed: 19 June 2013).

Høyblokka (2010–12) 'Høyblokka – Post Mortem'/'The Tower Block – Post Mortem'. Available at: http://www.hoyblokka.no/; http://www.hoyblokka.no/eng.php (Both accessed: 5 August 2012).

Hutcheon, L. (2009) 'Preface. creators and critics on adapting: learning about critical adaptation', in MacArthur, M., Wilkinson, L. and Zaiontz, K. (eds) *Performing Adaptations: Essays and Conversations on the Theory and Practice of Adaptation.* Newcastle upon Tyne: Cambridge Scholars Publishing, pp. xi–xiii. Available at: http://www.c-s-p.org/flyers/978-1-4438-0512-4-sample.pdf (Accessed: 20 January 2014).

Hutcheon, L. (with S. O'Flynn) (2013) *A Theory of Adaptation,* 2nd edn. New York: Routledge.

Hutchison, Y. (2005) 'Truth or bust: consensualising a historic narrative or provoking through theatre. The place of the personal narrative in the Truth and Reconciliation Commission'. *Contemporary Theatre Review.* 13(2), pp. 354–362.

Hutchison, Y. (2009) 'Verbatim theatre in South Africa: "living history in a person's performance"', in Forsyth, A. and Megson, C. (eds) *Get Real: Documentary Theatre Past and Present.* London: Palgrave Macmillan, pp. 209–223.

DOI: 10.1057/9781137577047.0009

Imploding Fictions (2011) *You Are Invited.* Available at: http://implodingfictions.wordpress.com/you-are-invited/ (Accessed: 18 January 2014).

Imploding Fictions (2014) Available at: http://www.implodingfictions.com/ (Accessed: 18 January 2014).

International Federation for Theatre Research (IFTR) (2012) *Intermediality in Theatre and Performance Working Group.* Available at: http://www.firt-iftr.org/working-groups/stage-forms/intermediality-in-theatre-and-performance (Accessed: 5 January 2014).

irc Theatre, Live!!! (1993) *About the Hamnet Players.* Available at: http://www.hambule.co.uk/hamnet/ (Accessed: 31 December 2013).

irc Theatre, Live!!! (1994a) 'The script'. *PCBeth: An IBM Clone of Macbeth.* Available at: http://www.hambule.co.uk/hamnet/pscript.htm (Accessed: 30 December 2013).

irc Theatre, Live!!! (1994b) 'Log of the actual performance'. *PCBeth: An IBM Clone of Macbeth.* 10 July. Available at: http://www.hambule.co.uk/hamnet/ (Accessed: 10 June 2013).

Jamieson, H. V. (2008) *Adventures in Cyberformance: Experiments at the Interface of Theatre and the Internet.* Unpublished Master of Arts (Research) Thesis. Australia: Queensland University of Technology. Available at: http://creative-catalyst.com/thesis.html; http://eprints.qut.edu.au/28544/1/Helen_Jamieson_Thesis.pdf (Accessed and downloaded: 5 January 2014).

Jamieson, H. V. (2012a) Interviewed by Christina Papagiannouli. 3 April. Available at: http://www.etheatre.info/e_theatre/Helen_Varley_Jamieson.html (Accessed: 4 January 2014).

Jamieson, H. V. (2012b) 'Tate webcast disappoints me ...', *Furtherfield Community Blog Stream.* 3 May. Available at: http://www.furtherfield.org/blog/helen-varley-jamieson/tate-webcast-disappoints-me (Accessed: 28 May 2013).

Jamieson, H. V. (2013a) *Cyberformance.* Available at: http://creative-catalyst.com/cyberformance/ (Accessed: 10 January 2014).

Jamieson, H. V. (2013b) Private email to Christina Papagiannouli, 14 August.

Jamieson, H. V. (2013c) Private email to Christina Papagiannouli, 14 October.

Jamieson, H. V. (2013d) Private email to Christina Papagiannouli, 19 October.

DOI: 10.1057/9781137577047.0009

Jezierska, K. (2011) *Radical Democracy Redux: Politics and Subjectivity beyond Habermas and Mouffe*. Örebro, Sweden: Örebro University. Available at: http://www.diva-portal.org/smash/get/diva2:406708/FULLTEXT01.pdf (Accessed: 16 January 2014).

Jones, E. (2000) *Constructing Transformative Spaces, Transforming Gendered Lives*. Unpublished MPhil Dissertation. Brighton, UK: Institute of Development Studies.

Jury, C. (2012) 'Creative activism as a resolution of the problem of political art as art'. *ATINER's Conference Paper Series No. ART2012-0072*. Athens: Athens Institute for Education and Research (ATINER). Available at: http://www.atiner.gr/papers/ART2012-0072.pdf (Accessed: 11 July 2013).

Kaplan, A. M. and Haenlein, M. (2009) 'Users of the world, unite! The challenges and opportunities of social media'. *Business Horizons*, 53(1), pp. 59–68.

Kaplan, E. W. (2005) 'Going the distance: trauma, social rupture, and the work of "repair" '. *Theatre Topics*, 15(2), pp. 171–183.

Kattenbelt, C. (2006) 'Theatre as the art of the performer and the stage of intermediality', in Freda, C. and Kattenbelt, C. (eds) *Intermediality in Theatre and Performance*. Amsterdam: Rodopi, pp. 29–40.

Kattenbelt, C. (2008) 'Intermediality in theatre and performance: definitions, perceptions and medial relationships'. *Cultural Studies Journal of Universitat Jaume I*, 5, pp. 19–29. Available at: http://www.e-revistes.uji.es/index.php/clr/article/viewFile/30/30 (Accessed: 20 January 2014).

Kattenbelt, C. (2010) 'Intermediality in performance and as a mode of performativity', in Bay-Cheng, S., Kattenbelt, C., Lavender, A. and Nelson, R. (eds) *Mapping Intermediality in Performance*. Amsterdam: Amsterdam University Press, pp. 29–37.

Katik, M. (2013) 'Turks deprived of TV turn to Twitter for protest news'. *BBC Monitoring*, 4 June. Available at: http://www.bbc.co.uk/news/world-europe-22756884 (Accessed: 19 June 2013).

Kershaw, B. (1992) *The Politics of Performance: Radical Theatre as Cultural Intervention*. Oxon and New York: Routledge.

Kershaw, B. (1999) *The Radical in Performance: Between Brecht and Baudrillard*. London and New York: Routledge.

Kershaw, B. (2000) 'The theatrical biosphere and ecologies of performance'. *New Theatre Quarterly*, 16, pp. 122–130.

DOI: 10.1057/9781137577047.0009

Kershaw, B. (2007) *Theatre Ecology: Environments and Performance Events.* Cambridge: Cambridge University Press.

King's Visualisation Lab (1999) *Theatron.* Available at: http://www.kvl. cch.kcl.ac.uk/theatron.html (Accessed: 17 January 2014).

Knowles, R. (2010) *Theatre & Interculturalism.* London and New York: Palgrave Macmillan.

Kobialka, M. (1999) *Of Borders and Thresholds: Theatre History, Practice, and Theory.* Minneapolis: University of Minnesota Press.

Kristeva, J. (1980) *Desire in Language: A Semiotic Approach to Literature and Art.* Edited and introduced by Leon S. Roudiez. New York: Columbia University Press.

La Pocha Nostra (2003–14) 'Gómez-Peña's La Pocha Nostra'. *La Pocha Nostra.* Available at: http://www.pochanostra.com/home/ (Accessed: 12 January 2014).

Laclau, E. and Mouffe, C. (1985) *Hegemony and Socialist Strategy: Towards a Radical Democratic Politics,* 2nd edn. London and New York: Verso.

Lanier, J. and Biocca, F. (1992) 'An insider's view of the future of virtual reality'. *Journal of Communication,* 42(4), pp. 150–172. Available at: http://www.mindlab.org/images/d/DOC812.pdf (Accessed: 10 January 2014).

Lavelli, J. (1996) 'Jorge Lavelli', in Delgado, M. M. and Heritage, P. (eds) *In Contact with the Gods?: Directors Talk Theatre.* Manchester and New York: Manchester University Press, pp. 106–128.

Lavender, A. (2006) 'Theatre and technology', in Luckhurst, M. (ed.) *A Companion to Modern British and Irish Drama, 1880–2005.* Oxford, UK: Blackwell Publishing, pp. 551–562.

Law, L. (2003) 'Transnational cyberpublics: new political spaces for labour migrants in Asia'. *Ethnic and Racial Studies,* 26(2), pp. 234–252. Available at: http://ldei.ugr.es/cddi/uploads/articulos/Law2003.pdf (Accessed: 5 December 2011).

Leavy, P. (2009) *Method Meets Art: Arts-Based Research Practice.* New York: The Guilford Press.

Lehmann, H. T. (2006) *Postdramatic Theatre.* Translated by Karen Jurs-Munby. New York: Routledge.

Leitch, T. (2005) 'Everything you always wanted to know about adaptation especially if you're looking forward rather than back'. *Literature/Film Quarterly,* 33(3), pp. 233–245. Available at: http://www. questia.com/library/journal/1P3-893589901/everything-you-always-wanted-to-know-about-adaptation (Accessed: 12 September 2013).

DOI: 10.1057/9781137577047.0009

Letsch, C. (2013) 'Social media and opposition to blame for protests, says Turkish PM'. *The Guardian* (Istanbul), 3 June. Available at: http://www.theguardian.com/world/2013/jun/02/turkish-protesters-control-istanbul-square (Accessed: 7 January 2014).

Livestream (2007) *About Livestream*. Available at: http://new.livestream.com/about/us (Accessed: 4 January 2014).

London International Festival of Theatre (LIFT) (2014) *About LIFT*. Available at: http://www.liftfestival.com (Accessed: 6 January 2014).

Lowen, M. (2012) 'Greeks ditch middleman to embrace "potato revolution" '. *BBC News* (Athens), 15 March. Available at: http://www.bbc.co.uk/news/world-europe-17369989 (Accessed: 6 January 2014).

MacArthur, M., Wilkinson, L. and Zaiontz, K. (2009) 'Introduction. Performing adaptations: the role of performance in adaptation studies', in MacArthur, M., Wilkinson, L. and Zaiontz, K. (eds) *Performing Adaptations: Essays and Conversations on the Theory and Practice of Adaptation*. Newcastle upon Tyne: Cambridge Scholars Publishing, pp. xvii–xxviii. Available at: http://www.c-s-p.org/flyers/978-1-4438-0512-4-sample.pdf (Accessed: 20 January 2014).

MacFarlane, J. (2000) 'Aristotle's definition of anagnorisis'. *American Journal of Philology*, 121(3), pp. 367–383.

*make-shift* (2010–14) Available at: http://make-shift.net/ (Accessed: 18 January 2014).

Martin, J. (2004) *The Intercultural Performance Handbook*. New York: Routledge.

Mayer, H. (1989) *Brecht on Stage*. A BBC Two Documentary directed by Amanda Willett. Available at: http://www.thedramateacher.com/brecht-on-stage-video/ (Accessed: 1 September 2013).

McGrath, J. E. (2012) 'Open culture: national theatre Wales'. *Watershed: Open City*. Available at: http://watershed.co.uk/opencity/wp-content/uploads/2012/03/National-Theatre-Wales-John-McGrath.pdf (Accessed: 10 May 2013).

McGrath J. E. (2013) Interviewed by Christina Papagiannouli. 8 October. Available at: http://etheatre.info/e_theatre/John_McGrath.html (Accessed: 14 January 2014).

McGrath, J. P. (1981) *The Cheliot, the Stag and the Black, Black Oil*. London: Methuen.

*Merry Crisis and a Happy New Fear* (2012) Directed by Christina Papagiannouli. 12:12:12, UpStage Festival, WaterWheel Tap.

DOI: 10.1057/9781137577047.0009

Performance log 12/12/12. Available at: http://www.etheatre.
info/e_theatre/Merry_Crisis_script.html (Accessed: 31 January 2014).

Merton (2014) *The Merton Show*. Available at: http://www.mertonshow.
com/ (Accessed: 16 January 2014).

Miessen, M. (2010) *The Nightmare of Participation (Crossbench Praxis as
a Mode of Criticality)*. Berlin: Sternberg Press. Available in part at:
http://www.sternberg-press.com/index.php?pageId=1270 (Accessed:
4 January 2014).

Mitchell, T. (1999) 'Terror at the terminal: how some artists view
computers', in Schrum, S. A. (ed.) *Theatre in Cyberspace: Issues of
Teaching, Acting and Directing*. New York: Peter Lang, pp. 9–18.

Mitter, S. (1992) *Systems of Rehearsal: Stanislavsky, Brecht, Grotowski and
Brook*. London and New York: Routledge.

Moi, T. (1986) *The Kristeva Reader: Julia Kristeva*. Oxford, UK: Basil
Blackwell.

Mosaika TV (2014) Available at: http://mosaika.tv/ (Accessed: 3 January
2014).

Mouffe, C. (1996) 'On the itineraries of democracy: an interview
with Chantal Mouffe'. *Studies in Political Economy*, 49(Spring), pp.
131–148. Available at: spe.library.utoronto.ca/index.php/spe/article/
download/9368/6320 (Accessed: 22 November 2013).

Mudford, P. (2000) *Making Theatre: From Text to Performance*. London
and New Jersey: Athlone Press.

Mudlark (2010) *Such Tweet Sorrow: *+ Lovers on Twitter for Five Weeks*.
Available at: https://vimeo.com/13130055 (Accessed: 18 May 2013).

Mumford, M. (2009) *Bertolt Brecht: Routledge Performance Practitioners*.
Oxon and New York: Routledge.

Mueller, R. (1987) 'Montage in Brecht'. *Theatre Journal*, 39(4), pp.
473–486.

Murray, J. H. (1997) *Hamlet on the Holodeck: The Future of Narrative in
Cyberspace*. New York: Free Press.

Naremore, J. (2000) 'Introduction: film and the reign of adaptation',
in Naremore, J. (ed.) *Film Adaptation*. New Brunswick, NJ: Rutgers
University Press, pp. 1–18.

National Theatre (2013–14) 'The National Theatre around the World:
National Theatre live'. *National Theatre*. Available at: http://www.
nationaltheatre.org.uk/support-us/american-associates-of-the-
national-theatre/the-national-theatre-around-the-world (Accessed:
9 June 2013).

DOI: 10.1057/9781137577047.0009

National Theatre Live (2009–14) 'About us'. *National Theatre Live.*
Available at: http://ntlive.nationaltheatre.org.uk/about-us (Accessed:
7 February 2014).

Near Now (2010–14) 'Field broadcast'. *Near Now: Technology in Everyday
Life.* Available at: http://nearnow.org.uk/people/field-broadcast/
(Accessed: 18 January 2014).

Nelson, R. (2010) 'Prospective mapping', in Bay-Cheng, S., Kattenbelt,
C., Lavender, A. and Nelson, R. (eds) *Mapping Intermediality in
Performance.* Amsterdam: Amsterdam University Press, pp. 13–23.

NESTA (2013–14) *Nesta: Innovation in the UK.* Available at: http://www.
nesta.org.uk/ (Accessed: 30 January 2013).

New Radio and Performing Arts, Inc. (NRPA) (1996) *Turbulence.* Available
at: http://turbulence.org/about/about.html (Accessed: 11 January 2014).

NTW (National Theatre Wales) (2009–10) *About National Theatre Wales.*
Available at: http://nationaltheatrewales.org/about# (Accessed: 10
May 2013).

NTW (National Theatre Wales) (2009–14) *National Theatre Wales
Community.* Available at: http://community.nationaltheatrewales.org/
(Accessed: 17 January 2014).

NTW (National Theatre Wales) (2010a) *National Theatre Wales Assembly.*
Available at: http://assembly.nationaltheatrewales.org/; http://www.
nationaltheatrewales.org/assembly (Both accessed: 17 January 2014).

NTW (National Theatre Wales) (2010b) *Love Steals Us from Loneliness.*
Available at: http://nationaltheatrewales.org/lovestealsus; http://
ourbridgend.com/ (Both accessed: 17 January 2014).

NTW (National Theatre Wales) (2011) *The Passion.* Available at: http://
www.nationaltheatrewales.org/passion (Accessed: 10 May 2013).

NTW (National Theatre Wales) (2012) *The Radicalisation of
Bradley Manning.* Available at: http://nationaltheatrewales.org/
bradleymanning (Accessed: 10 May 2013).

Nusberg, L. (1969) 'Cybertheater'. *Leonardo,* 2(1), pp. 61–62. Available
at: http://monoskop.org/images/e/e1/Nusberg,_Lev_(1969)_-_
Cybertheater.pdf (Accessed: 10 January 2014).

O'Loughlin, B., Boudeau, C. and Hoskins, A. (2011) 'Distancing
the extraordinary: audience understanding of discourses of
"radicalization" '. *Continuum: Journal of Media & Cultural Studies,*
25(2), pp. 153–164.

Oliver, M. (2013) 'Using mobile technologies in the performance
workshop' [PowerPoint presentation]. *Changing the Learning*

DOI: 10.1057/9781137577047.0009

*Landscape – Power in Your Pocket: The Creative Use of Mobile Technologies to Enhance Learning and Teaching in the Performing and Visual Arts.* Professional Development Workshop, University of Salford, Manchester, UK, 26 April. Available at: http://www. heacademy.ac.uk/events/detail/2013/24_April_CLL_Manchester (Accessed: 26 April 2013).

Palgrave Theatre (2013) '#quizoola'. *Twitter*, 13 April. Available at: https://twitter.com/search?q=%23quizoola&src=hash (Accessed: 25 June 2013).

Papagiannouli, C. (2011a) 'To be and not to be, that is the answer' [Abstract]. *Rethinking Intermediality in the Digital Age: Conference of the International Society for Intermedial Study*, 24–26 October 2013. Cluj-Napoca, Romania: Sapienta Hungarian University of Transylvania. Available at: http://film.sapientia.ro/uploads/oktatas/segedanyagok/2013. ISIS.Conf.Programme.pdf (Accessed: 5 January 2014).

Papagiannouli, C. (2011b) 'Cyberformance and the cyberstage'. *The International Journal of the Arts in Society*, 6(4), pp. 273–282. Available at: http://ija.cgpublisher.com/product/pub.85/prod.829 (Accessed: 5 January 2014).

Papagiannouli, C. (2012) 'Etheatre Project: the director as researcher'. *ATINER's Conference Paper Series No. ART2012-0172*. Athens: Athens Institute for Education and Research (ATINER). Available at: http://www.atiner.gr/papers/ART2012-0172.pdf (Accessed: 19 January 2014).

Papagiannouli, C. (2013a) 'Act 2: the revolution'. *CCC1*. Available at: http://www.youtube.com/watch?feature=player_embedded&v=BB_Xq5N3NFE (Accessed: 20 January 2014).

Papagiannouli, C. (2013b) 'Act 3: the secret marriage'. *CCC1*. Available at: http://www.youtube.com/watch?feature=player_embedded&v=hy7WjzZ_7no (Accessed: 20 January 2014).

Papagiannouli, C. (2013c) 'Etheatre Project III'. *Facebook*. Available at: https://www.facebook.com/groups/1424053814479386/ (Accessed: 23 November 2013).

Plaintext Players (1994–2006) *The Plaintext Players*. Available at: http://yin.arts.uci.edu/~players/index.html (Accessed: 10 June 2013).

Plaintext Players (1995) *LittleHamlet*. Available at: http://yin.arts.uci.edu/~players/hamlet.html (Accessed: 10 June 2013).

Popovich, G. (1999) 'Artaud unleashed: cyberspace meets the theatre of cruelty', in Schrum, S. A. (ed.) *Theatre in Cyberspace: Issues of Teaching, Acting and Directing*. New York: Peter Lang, pp. 221–237.

DOI: 10.1057/9781137577047.0009

Punchdrunk (2000–14) *Company: About, Company Structure, People.*
    Available at: http://punchdrunk.com/company (Accessed: 30
    December 2013).
Radosavljević, D. (2013) *Theatre-Making: Interplay Between Text and
    Performance in the 21st Century.* Basingstoke, UK: Palgrave Macmillan.
Rebellato, D. (2009) *Theatre & Globalization.* London and New York:
    Palgrave Macmillan.
Reynolds, J. (2010) 'Jacques Derrida (1930–2004)'. *Internet Encyclopedia
    of Philosophy: A Peer-Reviewed Academic Resource.* 12 January. Available
    at: http://www.iep.utm.edu/derrida/ (Accessed: 6 December 2013).
Rimini Protokoll (2002–14) *About Rimini Protokoll.* Available at: http://www.
    rimini-protokoll.de/website/en/about.html (Accessed: 15 January 2014).
Rimini Protokoll (2008–13) *Call Cutta in a Box: An Intercontinental
    Phone Play.* Available at: http://www.rimini-protokoll.de/website/en/
    project_2766.html (Accessed: 17 January 2014).
Royal Shakespeare Company (2010) *Special Projects: Such Tweet Sorrow.*
    Available at: http://www.rsc.org.uk/explore/projects/such-tweet-
    sorrow.aspx (Accessed: 30 December 2013).
Royal Shakespeare Company and Google+ (2013) *Midsummer Night's
    Dreaming: #dream40.* Available at: http://dream40.org/ (Accessed: 31
    December 2013).
Runcie, C. (2013) 'The Radicalisation of Bradley Manning: gripping
    portrayal of events leading to the US Army leaks'. *The List,* 20 August.
    Available at: http://edinburghfestival.list.co.uk/article/54113-the-
    radicalisation-of-bradley-manning/ (Accessed: 19 November 2013).
Sakellaridou, E. (2007) 'Millennial Artaud: rethinking cruelty and
    representation', in Detsi-Diamanti, Z., Kitsi-Mitakou, K. and
    Yiannopoulou, E. (eds) *The Flesh Made Text Made Flesh: Cultural and
    Theoretical Returns to the Body.* New York: Peter Lang, pp. 43–54.
Saltz, D. Z. (2004) 'Performing arts', in Schreibman, S., Siemens, R. and
    Unsworth. J. (eds) *A Companion to Digital Humanities.* Oxford, UK:
    Blackwell Publishing, pp. 121–131.
Sanders, J. (2006) *Adaptation and Appropriation: The New Critical Idiom.*
    New York: Routledge.
Savran, D. (1986) *Breaking the Rules: The Wooster Group.* New York:
    Theatre Communications Group.
Schechner, R. and Appel, W. (1990) 'Introduction', in Schechner, R. and
    Appel W. (eds) *By Means of Performance: Intercultural Studies in Theatre
    and Ritual.* Cambridge: Cambridge University Press, pp. 1–7.

DOI: 10.1057/9781137577047.0009

Schmid, A. P. (2013) 'Radicalisation, de-radicalisation, counter-radicalisation: a conceptual discussion and literature review'. *ICCT Research Paper*, March. The Hague, The Netherlands: International Centre for Counter-Terrorism (ICCT). Available at: http://www.icct.nl/download/file/ICCT-Schmid-Radicalisation-De-Radicalisation-Counter-Radicalisation-March-2013.pdf (Accessed: 22 November 2013).

Schoeps, K.-H. J. (1995) 'Bertolt Brecht and the Weimar Republic: rebel with a cause, or between Bacchant and Bolshevik', in Lyon, J. K. and Breuer, H. P. (eds) *Brecht Unbound: Presented at the International Bertolt Brecht Symposium Held at the University of Delaware, February 1992*. Newark/London: University of Delaware Press/Associated University Presses, pp. 43–62.

Schutzman M. (2006) 'Jok(e)ring: joker runs wild', in Cohen-Cruz, J. and Schutzman M. (eds) *A Boal Comparison: Dialogues on Theatre and Cultural Politics*. Oxon and New York: Routledge, pp. 133–145.

Scott, J. W. (1991) 'The evidence of experience'. *Critical Inquiry*, 17(4), pp. 773–797. Available at: http://www.jstor.org/discover/10.2307/1343743?uid=3738032&uid=2&uid=4&sid=21102938572533 (Accessed: 13 November 2013).

Second Life (1999–2014) Available at: http://secondlife.com/ (Accessed: 4 January 2014).

Shanken, E. A. (ed.) (2009) *Art and Electronic Media*. London and New York: Phaidon. Available at: http://artelectronicmedia.files.wordpress.com/2009/03/aem_preview_selections.pdf (Accessed: 7 January 2014).

Shirky, C. (2008) *Here Comes Everybody: The Power of Organizing without Organizations*. New York: Penguin.

Silberman, M. (1987) 'The politics of representation: Brecht and the media'. *Theatre Journal*, 39(4), pp. 448–460.

SL Shakespeare Company (2007–08) 'About'. *The SL Shakespeare Company*. Available at: http://slshakespeare.com/pages/about (Accessed: 10 June 2013).

SL Shakespeare Company (2009–10) 'About the company/Winter season *Twelfth Night*'. *SL Shakespeare Company Blog*. Available at: http://twelfthnight.slshakespeare.com/blog/about/ (Accessed: 10 June 2013).

Sobell, N. and Hartzell, E. (1994) *ParkBench: A History of Firsts on the Web*. Available at: http://www.cat.nyu.edu/parkbench/about.html (Accessed: 28 May 2013).

SPILL Festival of Performance (2007–14) Available at: http://www.
spillfestival.com/; http://spillfestival.com/resources/SPILL%202013.
pdf (Both accessed: 9 January 2014).

Stam, R. (2005) 'Introduction: the theory and practice of adaptation',
in Stam, R. and Raengo, A. (eds) *Literature and Film: A Guide to
the Theory and Practice of Film Adaptation*. Malden, MA: Blackwell
Publishing, pp. 1–52.

Stephens, S. (2013) '#quizoola24'. *Twitter*, 13 April. Available at: https://
twitter.com/StephensSimon/status/323094079430860803 (Accessed:
25 June 2013).

Subiotto, A. (1975) *Bertolt Brecht's Adaptations for the Berliner Ensemble*.
London: The Modern Humanities Research Association.

Tate (2011) *Tate and BMW Announce Major New International Partnership:
BMW Tate Live* [Press release]. 13 October. Available at: http://
www.tate.org.uk/about/press-office/press-releases/tate-and-
bmw-announce-major-new-international-partnership-bmw-tate
(Accessed: 28 May 2013).

Tate (2012) *BMW Tate Live: Performance Room 2012 artists' commissions
announced: Jérôme Bel, Pablo Bronstein, Harrell Fletcher, Joan Jonas
and Emily Roysdon* [Press release]. 22 February. Available at: http://
www.tate.org.uk/about/press-office/press-releases/bmw-tate-live-
performance-room-2012-artists-commissions-announced (Accessed:
28 May 2013).

Taylor, G. (1989) *Reinventing Shakespeare: A Cultural History from the
Restoration to the Present*. New York: Weidenfeld & Nicolson.

Terranova, T. (2000) 'Free labor: producing culture for the digital
economy'. *Social Text*, 18(2), pp. 33–58. Available at: http://muse.jhu.
edu/journals/soc/summary/v018/18.2terranova.html (Accessed:
6 December 2013).

Trueman, M. (2013) '#quizoola'. *Twitter*, 21 May. Available at: https://
twitter.com/search?q=%23quizoola&src=hash (Accessed: 25 June
2013).

Turner, Victor (1990) 'Are there universals of performance in myth,
ritual, and drama?', in Schechner, R. and Appel, W. (eds) *By Means
of Performance: Intercultural Studies in Theatre and Ritual*. Cambridge:
Cambridge University Press, pp. 8–18.

United Nations (2011) *Report of the Special Rapporteur on the Promotion
and Protection of the Right to Freedom of Opinion and Expression* (Frank
La Rue). Seventeenth Session of the Human Rights Council,

DOI: 10.1057/9781137577047.0009

16 May. Report No. A/HRC/17/27. Available at: http://www2.ohchr.
org/english/bodies/hrcouncil/docs/17session/A.HRC.17.27_en.pdf
(Accessed: 6 January 2014).

Unterman, B. (2005) *Computer-Mediated Theatre: An Examination of an
Emerging Art Form.* MA Thesis. Canada: University of Alberta.

Unterman, B. (2007) 'The audience in cyberspace: the lessons of
hyperformance'. Paper presented at the *Intermediality, Theatricality,
Performance, (Re)-presentation and the New Media Conference,* Ninth
International Conference of CRI and LANTISS, Montreal, Quebec,
Canada, 25–29 May. Abstract available at: http://cri.histart.umontreal.
ca/cri/fr/cdoc/fiche_activite.asp?id=1816 (Accessed: 26 January 2013).

UpStage (2004) *About UpStage.* Available at: http://upstage.org.nz/
blog/?page_id=2 (Accessed: 2 January 2014).

UpStage (2013) *Version 3 User Manual (DRAFT).* Available at: http://
upstage.org.nz/blog/wp-content/uploads/upstagev3usermanualdraft.
pdf (Accessed: 10 July 2014).

Velody, I. (1998) ' "The archive and the human sciences": notes towards
a theory of the archive'. *History of the Human Sciences (SAGE Journals),*
11, pp. 1–16.

Verhoeven, D. (2010) *Life Streaming.* Available at: http://www.
driesverhoeven.com/en/project/life-streaming (Accessed: 17 January
2014).

Verhoeven, D. (2012) Interviewed by Christina Papagiannouli. 22
February. Available at: http://etheatre.info/e_theatre/Dries_
Verhoeven.html (Accessed: 15 January 2014).

Virtual Vaudeville (2004) 'Virtual Vaudeville: the concept'. *The Virtual
Vaudeville Project.* Available at: http://www.virtualvaudeville.com/
concept.htm (Accessed: 14 January 2014).

VisitorsStudio (2003) *About VisitorsStudio.* Available at: http://www.
visitorsstudio.org/about_vs.html (Accessed: 3 January 2014).

Wagner, M. and Ernst, W.–D. (2010) 'Networking', in Bay-Cheng,
S., Kattenbelt, C., Lavender, A. and Nelson, R. (eds) *Mapping
Intermediality in Performance.* Amsterdam: Amsterdam University
Press, pp. 173–184.

Walsh, M. (2009) 'Manifesto'. *Futuretainment: Yesterday World Changed,
Now It's Your Turn.* New York: Phaidon.

Waterwheel Tap (2011) *About Waterwheel.* Available at: http://water-
wheel.net/ (Accessed: 3 January 2014).

DOI: 10.1057/9781137577047.0009

Weber, C. (2002) [1967] 'Brecht as director', in Schneider, R. and Cody, G. (eds) *Re: Direction: A Theoretical and Practical Guide*. London and New York: Routledge, pp. 84–89.

Weber, C. and Munk, E. (1967–68) 'Brecht as director'. *TDR*, 12(1), pp. 101–107.

WeHaveASituation (2013) Available at: http://www.wehaveasituation. net/ (Accessed: 18 January 2014).

Werber, N. (2003) 'Media theory after Benjamin and Brecht: neo-Marxist?', in Gumbrecht, H. U. and Marrinan, M. (eds) *Mapping Benjamin: The Work of Art in the Digital Age*. California: Stanford University Press, pp. 230–238.

White, E. J. (2009) 'Bakhtinian dialogism: a philosophical and methodological route to dialogue and difference?'. *Annual Conference of the Philosophy of Education Society of Australasia (PESA)*, Honolulu, Hawaii, 3–6 December, pp. 1–18. Available at: http://www2.hawaii. edu/~pesaconf/zpdfs/16white.pdf (Accessed: 18 September 2013).

White, G. (2013) *Audience Participation in Theatre: Aesthetics of the Invitation*. Basingstoke, UK and New York: Palgrave Macmillan.

White, M. (2006) *The Body and the Screen: Theories of Internet Spectatorship*. London: MIT Press.

Whitmore, J. (1994) *Directing Postmodern Theatre: Shaping Signification in Performance*. Ann Arbor: University of Michigan Press.

Wiens, B. (2010) 'Instance: Christopher Kondek, *Dead Cat Bounce* (2005)', in Bay-Cheng, S., Kattenbelt, C., Lavender, A. and Nelson, R. (eds) *Mapping Intermediality in Performance*. Amsterdam: Amsterdam University Press, pp. 101–108.

Wilde, O. (2007) [1891] *The Critic as Artist (With Some Remarks upon the Importance of Doing Nothing)*. Edited by Andrew Moore. New York: Mondial.

Williams, H. (2013) 'Edinburgh 2013: *The Radicalisation of Bradley Manning* – Tim Price's play is a sympathetic portrait of the Wiki-leaker'. *The Independent*, 20 August. Available at: http://www. independent.co.uk/arts-entertainment/theatre-dance/reviews/ edinburgh-2013-the-radicalisation-of-bradley-manning--tim-prices-play-is-a-sympathetic-portrait-of-the-wikileaker-8775833.html (Accessed: 18 October 2013).

Wolff, R. (2010) 'Capitalist crisis and the return to Marx: the rise, fall, and return of Marxian analyses'. *Professor Richard D. Wolff*, 18 March.

DOI: 10.1057/9781137577047.0009

Available at: http://rdwolff.com/content/capitalist-crisis-and-return-marx (Accessed: 9 August 2012).

Wooster Group, The (2006–13) *Hamlet.* Available at: http://thewoostergroup.org/twg/twg.php?hamlet (Accessed: 9 June 2013).

Wurtzler, S. (1992) 'She sang live, but the microphone was turned off: the live, the recorded, and the subject of representation', in Altman, R. (ed.) *Sound Theory Sound Practice.* New York and London: Routledge, pp. 87–103.

Wysing Arts Centre (2008–14) *Overview.* Available at: http://www.wysingartscentre.org//about/overview (Accessed: 18 January 2014).

DOI: 10.1057/9781137577047.0009

# List of Websites

## A.1   Etheatre project

Website: http://www.etheatre.info/
Scoop it: http://www.scoop.it/t/etheatre
Twitter: https://twitter.com/e_theatre
*Cyberian Chalk Circle*: http://www.etheatre.info/e_theatre/
Cyberian_Chalk_Circle.html
*Cyberian Chalk Circle 1*: https://www.youtube.com/
watch?v=Ij7VedHe6jc
*Cyberian Chalk Circle 2*: https://www.youtube.com/
watch?v=EjqyrdKzXEw
*Cyberian Chalk Circle 3*: https://www.youtube.com/
watch?v=QzXeChv7MJ4
*Merry Crisis and a Happy New Fear*: http://www.etheatre.
info/e_theatre/Merry_Crisis_%26_a_Happy_New_
Fear.html
*Merry Crisis and a Happy New Fear 1*: https://www.youtube.
com/watch?v=UlZXT9tH_So
*Merry Crisis and a Happy New Fear 2*: https://www.youtube.
com/watch?v=yjCbtEWDe6g
*Etheatre Project and Collaborators*: http://www.etheatre.
info/e_theatre/Etheatre_%26_Collaborators.html
*Etheatre Project and Collaborators 1*: http://www.youtube.
com/watch?v=BX2ZsbjNjZM
*Etheatre Project and Collaborators 2*: http://www.youtube.
com/watch?v=u35rCAxRJUo

DOI: 10.1057/9781137577047.0010

## A.2   Artists and companies

Avatar Body *Collision*: http://www.avatarbodycollision.org/
Blast Theory: http://www.blasttheory.co.uk/
BMW Tate Room: http://www.tate.org.uk/whats-on/tate-modern/
   eventseries/bmw-tate-live
Desktop Theatre: http://www.desktoptheater.org/
Dries Verhoeven: http://www.driesverhoeven.com/
Field Broadcast: http://www.fieldbroadcast.org
Forced Entertainment: http://www.forcedentertainment.com/
Hamnet Players: http://www.hambule.co.uk/hamnet/
Imploding Fictions: http://www.implodingfictions.com/
Merton: http://www.mertonshow.com/
National Theatre Wales (NTW): http://www.nationaltheatrewales.org/
   about
ParkBench: http://www.cat.nyu.edu/parkbench/
Plaintext Players: http://yin.arts.uci.edu/~players/
Punchdrunk: http://punchdrunk.com/
Rimini Protokoll: http://www.rimini-protokoll.de/website/en/
Royal Shakespeare Company (RSC): http://www.rsc.org.uk/
SL Shakespeare Company: http://slshakespeare.com/

## A.3   Projects and performances

*Angry Women*: http://www.bram.org/angry/women/
*Call Cutta in a Box*: http://www.rimini-protokoll.de/website/en/
   project_2766.html
*Dream40*: http://dream40.org/
*Høyblokka*: http://www.hoyblokka.no/
*La Pocha Nostra*: http://www.pochanostra.com/
*Life Streaming*: http://www.driesverhoeven.com/en/project/life-streaming
*make-shift*: http://make-shift.net/
*Net Congestion*: http://www.robat.scl.net/content/PaiPres/presencesite/
   html/dixchamel.html
NTW Assembly: http://www.nationaltheatrewales.org/assembly
NTW Community blog: http://community.nationaltheatrewales.org/
NTW, *Love Steals Us from Loneliness*: http://nationaltheatrewales.org/
   lovestealsus; http://ourbridgend.com/

DOI: 10.1057/9781137577047.0010

NTW, *The Passion*: http://port-talbot.com/
NTW, *The Radicalisation of Bradley Manning*: http://nationaltheatrewales.
  org/bradleymanning
*Quizoola24!*: http://www.forcedentertainment.com/page/3102/24-hour-
  Quizoola
*Theatron Project*: http://www.kvl.cch.kcl.ac.uk/theatron.html
*Turbulence*: http://turbulence.org/about/about.html
*You Are Invited*: http://implodingfictions.wordpress.com/you-are-invited/
*Virtual Vaudeville*: http://www.virtualvaudeville.com/
*We Have a Situation*: http://www.wehaveasituation.net/

## A.4   Platforms

Chatroulette: http://chatroulette.com/
DownStage: https://trac.foobarlab.net/downstage
eTV: https://www.etv.org.nz/v4/aboutetv.php
Livestream: http://new.livestream.com/
Mosaika.tv: http://www.mosaika.tv/
Second Life: http://secondlife.com/
UpStage: http://upstage.org.nz/blog/
Visitors Studio: http://www.visitorsstudio.org/?diff=0
Waterwheel Tap: http://water-wheel.net

## A.5   Art centres, festivals and archives

Anywhere Theatre Festival: http://anywherefest.com/
APO33: http://www.apo33.org/
Bikeshed Theatre: http://www.bikeshedtheatre.co.uk/
Centre Régional D'Art Contemporain Languedoc-Roussillon:
  http://crac.languedocroussillon.fr/3171-archives-expositions-art-
  contemporain-crac-sete.htm
Furtherfield Gallery: http://furtherfield.org/gallery
Govett Brewster Gallery: http://www.govettbrewster.com/
Kunstraum Goethestrasse: http://www.kunstraum.at/
London International Festival of Theatre (LIFT): http://www.liftfestival.
  com/
MAD Emergent Art Centre: http://madlab.nl/

DOI: 10.1057/9781137577047.0010

Marionet Theatro: http://www.marioneteatro.com/
New Zealand Film Archive: http://www.filmarchive.org.nz/
Piet Zwart Institute: http://www.pzwart.nl/
Schaumbad Freies Atelierhaus Graz: http://web455.webbox333.server-
    home.org/
Signalraum: http://www.signalraum.de/sig/programm.html
SPILL Festival: http://www.spillfestival.com/
Werkstatt am Hauptplatz: http://werkstatt-am-hauptplatz.at/
Wysing Arts Centre: http://www.wysingartscentre.org/

## A.6    Performance videos

*Angry Women*: *https://www.youtube.com/watch?v=swnrP9KpN8s*
*Call Cutta in a Box*: http://www.youtube.com/watch?v=mAjK4PQOhoM
*Field Broadcast*: https://vimeo.com/32434578
*Life Streaming*: http://www.youtube.com/watch?v=jZ5mhPgTFaI
*Mertonian Chatroulette*: http://www.youtube.com/watch?v=JTwJetox_tU
*Ode to Merton*: https://www.youtube.com/watch?v=LfamTmY5REw
*Such Tweet Sorrow*: https://vimeo.com/13130055
*You Are Invited (Norway)*: http://www.youtube.com/watch?v=-
    CBzr9dSY1c

DOI: 10.1057/9781137577047.0010

# Index

Abrahams, Annie, 22, 33–34,
   41–42, 85
activist theatre, 23, 26, 35, 40–42
actor-network theory, Latour,
   58–59
adaptation
   antistrophe, 52
   contextual, 50–51
   cyber-, *Cyberian Chalk Circle*,
      45, 49–62, 84
   intermedial, 50
   technology, 10–11
agora, 14–15, 24
anagnorisis, 59–60
*Angry Women* (Abrahams), 22,
   33–35, 41, 85, 114, 116
Anywhere Theatre Festival, 34,
   42n2, 115
APO$_{33}$, 39, 81, 115
Arab Spring, 16
archive space, 21, 23, 37, 86, 115
archivization, 23, 36–37, 41, 86
Aristotle, 7, 24, 59
Artaud, Antonin, *xii–xiii*,
   *xvi–xvii*
Auslander, Philip, 9
Avatar Body *Collision*
   (company), 5, 6, 114

Baer, Ralph H., 80
Bakhshi, Hasan, 12
Bakhtin, Mikhail, 46, 51
Ball, Mark, 2, 9, 29
Ban Ki-moon, 73
Beacham, Richard, 32

Beardshaw, Tom, 27
Beaudry, Jeremy, 20
Benjamin, Walter, 15
Bikeshed Theatre, 81, 115
Birch, Rebecca, 40
Bishop, Clare, 20, 40, 41
Blandford, Steve, 26
Blast Theory, *xiv*, 114
*BMW Tate Live: Performance
   Room*, 2, 114
Boal, Augusto, 48, 55, 67
bodyless, characteristic of
   cyberstage, *xvii*, 7, 32, 38,
   48, 75
Bolter, Jay David, *xiv*
Brager, Øystein Ulsberg, 22,
   34–35, 41, 85
Brecht, Bertolt, 8
   audience engagement, 55–58
   *The Caucasian Chalk Circle*,
      49, 51–52
   clown, 56, 70
   directing, *xviii–xix*, 48–49
   improvisation, 55
   montage theory, 64
   *Mother Courage and Her
      Children*, 46
   political theatre, *xviii*, 45–53,
      81, 84
   radio, 13–15, 17
   spect-actor, 48–49, 55, 67, 69
   Stanislavsky, 53, 55
Brechtian, 21, 44–52, 55–56, 67,
   69–70, 75, 81 84, 86–87
Brenneis, Lisa, *xv*

Brook, Peter, 48
Burton, Richard, 11

*Call Cutta in a Box* (Rimini Protokoll),
    *xviii*, 22, 41, 85, 114, 116
Cartledge, Paul, 25
Case, Sue-Ellen, 37
Castelyn, Sarahleigh, 68
*Caucasian Chalk Circle, The* (Brecht),
    49, 51–52
Causey, Matthew, *xi–xii*, *xvii*, 11
C-effect (cultural distance), 53
Centre Régional D'Art Contemporain
    Languedoc-Roussellon, 34, 115
*Chameleons 3: Net Congestion*
    (Chameleons Group), *xii*
chat box, 22, 28, 38–39, 42, 45, 47, 55,
    59, 62, 66, 68, 73, 75, 77, 79–81,
    86–87, 89
Chatroulette, 37, 38, 43n3, 116
Chatzichristodoulou, Maria, *xiii*, *xvi*, 2, 5
clown, Brecht's, 56, 70
Collinge, Geraldine, 5
community theatre, Kershaw's
    definition, 20–21
conflictual participation, 20, 24–25, 45,
    85–88
Cross, Ann, 63, 66, 68
Crutchlow, Paula, 38
cyberculture, 6, 17, 77
cyberdrama, *xi*, *xvi*
cyber-ethnography, 62, 64
cyber-ethnotheatre
    directing methodology, 45, 49, 86
    *Merry Crisis and a Happy New Fear*,
        62–67
cyberformance
    2012 as year of, 84
    bodyless, 7, 32, 38, 48, 75
    community, 21–22
    definition, *xv–xvi*, 6–7
    genre, *x*
    interactivity, 10–13, 45, 84
    liveness, *xvii*, *xviii*, 7, 9, 10–13, 48,
        64, 84
    participation, 79

as a performative, 13–17
spaceless, 7, 32, 36, 38, 48, 57, 75
as theatre, 6–10
*Cyberian Chalk Circle* (Etheatre
    Project), *xviii*, 42, 45
collaborations, 67–69
cyber-adaptation, 49–62
cyberstage, 57, 75
Etheatre Project research, 81
factual production circumstances, 87
real-timeadaptation, 56–57, 86
'safe scenes', 62
screenshots, 76, 78
staging, 58–62
text log of Part B, 54
cyberperformance, *xi*
cyber-street theatre, 23, 35–37, 41–42, 86
cybertheater(s)/cyber(-)theatre,
    *xi–xiii*, *xvi*
'cyber turn' introducing, 2–6
CyPosium, 6, 84

Dahlberg, Lincoln, 15, 25
Danet, Brenda, 3
Deleuze, Gilles, *xiii*, 63
Derrida, Jacques, 23, 36–37, 47
Desktop Theatre, 114
devise, collaborative improvisation, 53
dialectics/dialectical
    cyberformance, *xix*, 42, 69, 89
    methodologies, 57
    participation, 20, 45, 66, 75, 81, 86–87
    spectator, 20, 47–49
    theatre, Brecht, 14–15, 51, 69
dialogism, 50, 51
digital performance, *x*, *xi*, *xv*, *xvi*
distancing effect, *see* V-effect
    (*Verfremdungeffekt*)
Dixon, Steve, *xii*, 7, 11, 22, 32, 41
domestic theatre, 23, 35–36
Donzi, Anca, 68
DownStage (platform), 5, 115
DPA (Digital Performance Archive), 7
*Dream4o* (performance), 2, 84, 114

ecology, 39–40

Egypt
  *Cyberian Chalk Circle*, 50, 53, 55,
    60–61, 87
  political use of Internet, 16, 77–78, 84
  revolution in, 68, 80
El Baroni, Bassam, 20
English, James F., 21
Erdogan, Recep, 17
Etheatre Project, *x*, 2, 8, 22, 42, 113
  co-presence embodiment on
    cyberstage, 75–81
  cyber-adaptation, 49–62
  cyber-collaboration, 67–74
  cyber-ethnotheatre, 62–67
  directing methodologies, 45
  participation and interaction, 88–89
  political spaces, 86–87
*Etheatre Project and Collaborators*
    (Etheatre Project), *xviii*, 42, 45, 113
  audience involvement, 86–87
  cyber-collaboration, 67–74
  migration and improvisation, 87–88
  screenshot, 74
  eTV (platform), 6, 115

*fabel* (fabie), 46
Facebook, 13–14, 16–17, 37, 58–59, 61, 67,
    70–71, 75, 79–80
Feral, Josette, 30
Field Broadcast (platform), 23, 40–42,
    86, 114, 116
Folds, Ben, 23, 37, 86
Forced Entertainment, *xiv*, 2, 10, 12–13,
    27, 84, 115
Freedom Theatre in Palestine, 27
Fuks, Suzon, 39–40, 68
Furtherfield Gallery, 2, 34, 39, 115

Gavriilidis, Charis, 68
*Gestus*, 46, 48, 77, 89
Giannachi, Gabriella, *xiv*
Gielgud, John, 11
Google, 16, 31, 53, 58, 80, 82*n*2
Google+, 2–3
Gorky, Maxim, 52
Govett Brewster Gallery, 81, 115

Green, Jo-Anne, *xiii*
Grotowski, Jerzy, 9
Grusin, Richard, *xiv*
Guattari, Felix, *xiii*

*Hamnet* (Hamnet Players), 2, 4, 84
Hamnet Players, 2–4, 84, 114
Haraway, Donna, 5
Hare, David, 64
Harris, Stuart, 3–4
Hartzell, Emily, 2
Haug, Helgard, 32, 33
H-effect (historicization), 46, 52
heteroglossia, 51
Høyblokka Project, 21, 23, 36–38, 41,
    86, 114
Hutcheon, Linda, 50
hybridity, 30, 51, 53
hyperformance, *xi*, *xv*, *xvi*

IFTR (International Federation of
    Theatre Research), 7
*Imploding Fictions*, 34, 114
in-between space, 6–8, 41, 45, 47–49,
    53, 55, 67, 69, 75, 81, 84, 89
interactivity, cyberformance, 10–13,
    45, 84
interculturalism, 22, 29–35, 42
  intermedial, 29–35
intermediality, 7–8
Intermediality in Theatre and
    Performance Working Group, 7
Internet
  communication, *x*
  platforms for theatre production,
    *x–xi*
  political power, 15–17, 77–78, 84
*Internet Street Theatre*, *xv*
intertextuality, 51
IRC (Internet relay chat), 3–4
irc Theatre, 2–4

Jamieson, Helen Varley, *xv*, 2, 3, 5, 6, 8,
    21, 24, 38–39, 42, 67, 71, 86
Jenik, Adrienne, *xv*
Jury, Christopher, 40–41

•

DOI: 10.1057/9781137577047.0011

Kaegi, Stefan, 32
Kaplan, Ellen W., 21
Kattenbelt, Chiel, 9–10, 55, 67
Kershaw, Baz, 15–16, 20–21, 40
Klinkhamer, Marischka, 68
Kunstraum Goethestrasse, 81, 115

language, communication, 78–79
Latour, Bruno, 58
Lavender, Andy, *xvi*, 6
Law, Lisa, 75, 78
L-effect (foreign-language distancing), 79
*Life Streaming* (Verhoeven), *xviii*, 22,
    29–35, 85, 114, 116
LIFT (London International Festival of
    Theatre), 2, 30, 115
Little Hamlet (Plaintext Players), 4–5
liveness, cyberformance, 7, 9, 10–13, 48,
    64, 84
Livestream (platform), 6, 115
Li Xingdao, 51
*Love Steals Us from Loneliness* (NTW),
    28, 114

McGrath, John E., 20, 25–29
McGrath, John P., 21
McLuhan, Marshall, 20
MAD Emergent Art Centre, 39, 115
*make-shift*, 38, 114
Mangan, Tom, 63, 66, 68
Manning, Bradley, 22, 28–29, 85, 115
Marlow, Bethan, 3
Martin, John, 29, 30
Marxism, 48, 51
Mayer, Han, 47
memory, 57, 80
    archive space, 36–37, 86
    public, 41
    world or globalized, 63
*Merry Crisis and a Happy New Fear*
    (Etheatre Project), *xviii*, 42, 45, 113
    audience participation, 86–87
    cyber-collaboration, 67–70, 73, 82*n*3
    cyber-ethnotheatre, 62–67
    equality in cyberformance, 89
Merton, 23, 37–38, 41, 86

Mertonian Chatroulette, 37, 38, 116
Miessen, Markus, 15–16, 20, 24, 49
migration, 42, 70–74, 87
Mitchell, Twyla, 8
MOOS (multi-user object-oriented), 3, 4
Morrison, Howard J., 80
mosaika.tv (platform), 6, 115
Mouffe, Chantal, 16, 24–25, 27
Müller, Heiner, 5
Murphy, Paul, *xii*
Murray, Janet H., *xi*

Nelson, Robin, 9, 20
Net.art, *xixn*1
networked performance, *xiii*, *xvi*
new journalism, 64
NTLive Project, 2, 10–13, 18*n*1, 25,
    27–29, 84
NTW (National Theatre Wales), *xviii*,
    21, 25–29, 36, 41–42, 71, 114–15
    Assembly programme, 22, 26, 27, 114
    Community blog, *xviii*, 22, 26, 27,
        85, 114
    radicalization of, 23–29

online journalism, 64
Owen, Gary, 28

ParkBench (company), 2, 114
participation, 20, 23–24
    audience/spectator, 49, 57, 62, 66–67,
        70, 81, 87
    conflictual, 20, 24–25, 45, 85–88
    critical, 21, 47–49, 67, 75, 85, 87
    cyberformance, 79
    Internet, 20–23, 30, 40–42, 85, 87
    pseudo-, 20, 24
    radical, 23, 49, 88
    real-time interaction, 9. 11, 35, 84
participatory democracy, 15, 20–22, 24
*Passion, The* (NTW), 28, 115
*PCBeth: An IBM Clone of Macbeth*
    (Hamnet Players), 4
perfect spectator, 82*n*1
*Phédre* (NTLive's production), 2, 10–12,
    28, 84

DOI: 10.1057/9781137577047.0011

Plaintext Players (company), 2, 4–5, 114
pluralism, 20–21, 24
political cyberformance, 45
    directing, 86, 88
    engagement, 79, 88
    protecting identities of participants, 85
    real-time improvisation, 66–67
    UpStage, 71, 73
political debate, online discussion, 20
political power, Internet, 15–17, 77–78, 84
politicization, 51
postorganic performance, *xiii*
potato revolution, 16
Price, Tim, 28
pseudo-participation, 20, 24
Punchdrunk (company), 2, 26, 114

*Quizoola*, Forced Entertainment, 10,
    12–13, 27, 84, 115

radical democracy, 15, 22–25, 29–30,
    41–42
*Radicalisation of Bradley Manning, The*
    (NTW), 22, 28–29, 85, 115
radicalization, 22
    National Theatre Wales, 23–29
    theatre and Internet, 35
radical participation, 23, 49, 88
Radosavljević, Duška, 64
real-time improvisation, 55, 73, 88
Reed, Wendy, *xii*
Remembrance Day celebrations,
    60, 68
representation
    cyberculture, 77
    live, 8
    media, 21, 85
    online space as, of real, 75
    of reality, 17
    theatre, 58
    video, 65
Rial, Michelle, *xiii–xiv*
Rimini Protokoll (company), *xviii*,
    20–22, 26, 32, 85, 114
*Romeo and Juliet* (Twitter adaptation),
    2, 3, 5

Royal National Theatre, *xviii*, 2, 11,
    18*n*1, 31, 84
RSC (Royal Shakespeare Company),
    2–5, 84, 114
Runcie, Charlotte, 28

safe scenes, 62
Saltz, David Z., *xv–xvi*
scenography, 9, 31–32, 89
Schutzman, Mady, 21, 85
Second Life (platform), 2–3, 5–6, 75,
    81, 115
Sheen, Michael, 28
Shirky, Clay, 29
Siapera, Eugenia, 15, 25
Silberman, Marc, 56
Silbert, Roxana, 3
Skype, 21–23, 31, 33–34, 49, 58, 70, 72
SL Shakespeare Company, 2, 5, 114
Smith, Barry, 7
Smith, Rob, 40
Smith, Vicki, 5, 71
Sobell, Nina, 2
social dialogue, 46–47
social movement, definition, 16
social networking platforms, 10, 85
Sontag, Susan, 82*n*1
spaceless, characteristic of cyberstage,
    7, 32, 36, 38, 48, 57, 75
spect-actor
    Boal's, 48, 55, 67
    Brecht's, 48, 55, 67, 69
spectating, 47, 55–56, 69
spectators
    act of being, 47, 49, 56–57, 70
    communication with performers,
        78–79, 87–89
    dialectical participation, 20, 45, 86
    involvement in performance, 22, 32,
        46–47
    non-realistic staging, 46
    participation, 65, 81
    perfect, 82*n*1
SPILL Festival of Performance, 12,
    18*n*4, 116
Stamatiou, Evi, 49, 55, 67–68, 77, 79, 87

DOI: 10.1057/9781137577047.0011

Stanislavsky, Konstantin, 47, 53, 55, 87
stream scene, 49, 53, 62
*Such Tweet Sorrow* (Twitter
    performance), 2, 3, 5, 28, 84, 116

Tahrir Square, Cairo, 15, 77
Taksim Square, Istanbul, 15, 17
technology, online theatre, 10–11
telematic
    collaboration, *xvi*
    performance, *xi, xv–xvi*
telepresent performance, *xiii*
Terranova, Tiziana, 40
text box, 47, 57, 58, 64, 68, 70, 76–77
Thatcher, Margaret, *x*
theatre, 2, 6–10, 18*n*2
Theatron Project, 32, 115
Thorington, Helen, *xiii–xiv*
Thorne, Philip, 34
Throsby, David, 12
Todorut, Ilinca Tamara, 68, 72
*Training for a Better World* (Abrahams),
    34
Tsinikoris, Prodromos, 49, 67, 80
Turbulence Project, *xiii, xixn*1
Turner, Victor W., 8

UFF (Unidentified Flying Food), 39
Unterman, Benjamin, *xv*
UpStage Festival, *xvii*, 5–6, 34, 60, 68,
    81, 84
UpStage (platform), *xvi–xvii*, 5–6, 8, 23,
    38, 42, 115
    audience in setting, 80–81
    cyber-collaboration, 67–73
    *Cyberian Chalk Circle*, 49, 55, 59–61,
        67–68
    drawing tools, 77, 89
    plot development, 77
    political space, 86

presence in cyberformance, 75–80

V-effect (*Verfremdungeffekt*), 45, 47–48,
    51, 53, 57, 64, 68, 75, 77
Velody, Irving, 37
verbatim theatre, 42, 48, 63–65,
    86–87
Verhoeven, Dries, *xviii*, 20–22, 30–32,
    85, 114
violence, 17, 23, 54, 57
virtual reality, *xvi*
virtual theatre(s), *xi, xiv, xvi*
virtual touch, 22, 32–33, 42, 85
Virtual Vaudeville Project, *xv*
VisitorsStudio (platform), 6, 115

Wagner, Meike, 58–59
Waterwheel Tap (platform), 6, 8, 23,
    39–40, 115
    cyber-collaboration, 67–70
    *Cyberian Chalk Circle*, 49, 62
    drawing tools, 39, 89
    sense of audience in setting, 80
    technical rehearsals, 65
webcam
    avatar, 61, 69, 75, 80
    conversation, 43*n*3, 50
    cyberperformers, 75–77, 80
    live-streaming, 39, 87
    performance, 33
    technology of, 65–66, 68–69
Wetzel, Daniel, 32
Whitmore, Jon, 46
Willemen, Paul, 82*n*1
Wolf-Dieter, Ernst, 58–59
Wright, Tim, 3
Wysing Arts Centre, 40, 116

*You Are Invited* (Skype), 22–23, 34–35,
    41, 85, 115

DOI: 10.1057/9781137577047.0011

Lightning Source UK Ltd.
Milton Keynes UK
UKOW01n1031050216

267812UK00007B/192/P